ABOVE WATER

Trish Kearney is a writer and mother to five living in Cork, Ireland. Her weekly 'It's My Life' column ran in the *Irish Examiner* for over two years. She also has a popular blog, 'My Thoughts on a Page', and was awarded Best Personal Blog and Best Writer at the Irish Parenting Blog Awards in 2015.

Above Water is her first book.

ABOVE WATER

A Stolen Childhood
An Enduring Scandal
A Survivor's Story

Trish Kearney

HACHETTE
BOOKS
IRELAND

Copyright © 2021 Trish Kearney

First published in Ireland in 2021 by Hachette Books Ireland
First published in paperback in 2022

The right of Trish Kearney to be identified as the author of
the work has been asserted by her in accordance with the
Copyright, Designs and Patents Act 1988.

All rights reserved. No part of this publication may be reproduced,
stored in a retrieval system, or transmitted, in any form or by any
means without the prior written permission of the publisher, nor
be otherwise circulated in any form of binding or cover other than
that in which it is published and without a similar condition being
imposed on the subsequent purchaser.

Cataloguing in Publication Data is available from the British Library

ISBN 978 1 52933 366 4

Typeset in Adobe Garamond Pro by Bookends Publishing Services
Printed and bound in Great Britain by Clays Ltd, Elcograf S.p.A.

Author photograph © Rob Lambe

Hachette Books Ireland policy is to use papers that are natural,
renewable and recyclable products and made from wood grown
in sustainable forests. The logging and manufacturing processes
are expected to conform to the environmental regulations
of the country of origin.

Hachette Books Ireland
8 Castlecourt Centre
Castleknock
Dublin 15, Ireland

A division of Hachette UK Ltd
Carmelite House
50 Victoria Embankment, EC4Y 0DZ

www.hachettebooksireland.ie

For Mum and Dad

Contents

Prologue

The Start of Goodbye

It is 31 December 2018 and my husband Eamonn and I spend the final morning of the year packing for a couple of nights away in Mum's house, or 108 as we affectionately call my childhood home in Dublin. I'd left its comforts for Cork almost thirty years ago, when Eamonn and I married. In 108, along with my 87-year-old mum, and my cousin Eileen, we will ring in the New Year. Our grown children are of an age to make their own New Year plans and are eager to see us off.

I give each of them a kiss and we say our goodbyes. As I sit into the car and pull the door closed, I reach down as if to fix my shoelace, unable to look them in the eye as they wave us off from the door, for fear my veneer of faux happiness will slip. Ours will be nothing like the New Year they have planned. We drive off in silence as I know that if I open my mouth, the sobs I am holding back will escape. Thankfully, after three decades together, Eamonn hears what I cannot say. 2019 is fast approaching, the year that will take Mum from us.

I know this, but I wonder, does she? Mum is running out of steam. Recurring infections are weakening her. In the past twelve months she has broken her ribs, her shoulder and her hip. She has missed my younger brother Michael's wedding, and spent four months in hospital. Yet, I remind myself, she is still here. I must try to keep that as my focus.

A few hours later, I open the door to 108 and inhale the scent of my childhood. As a teenager, my swimming medals and trophies had been proudly displayed in the hall and all available shelves, and the sitting room walls were festooned with family photos of my two brothers, Ben and Michael, two sisters, Doris and Caroline and our cousin Eileen, who lives with Mum, and has taken on much of the caring for her in the last two years.

With the passing of time, my medals have relocated to a cupboard in my home in Cork, and First Communion and Confirmation photos have been replaced with those of graduations and grandchildren, forever reminders of many happy, joyful days in 108.

I greet Eileen, also my beloved godmother, who has been with Mum since her own mother died when she was a baby, 11 years before I was born. We go into the kitchen where Mum sits, her tiny frame dwarfed by the size of her chair. She is wearing the pale blue jumper I love, her obligatory pearls around her neck. Not one snow-white hair is out of place and her make-up and lipstick are perfectly applied. I match her broad smile of welcome, delighted to see her looking so well. She throws out her arms and, as I bend towards her, she enfolds me in a hug. It's only been ten days since my last visit, but her welcome is as warm and enthusiastic as if I'd returned from months abroad. We hold each other longer than we used to, as I inhale the sweet scent of Estée Lauder. Stepping aside, I let Eamonn through and can almost hear Mum purr as he says, 'Agnes, you look terrific.'

There is much chat and catching up to do as Christmas has come and gone since last we met. At her usual bedtime of nine o'clock, I note that she makes no move to go to bed, and as the New Year approaches she is still up. I smile. *2019, she is determined to stay up and look you direct in the eye.*

At the stroke of midnight, we clink glasses around her chair, but I struggle to celebrate, the words 'Happy New Year' sticking in my throat. For a moment I panic, battling tears, which collectively I sense we are not entertaining. Holding my breath, I lean forward to kiss Mum. She holds her head up high and smiles. No trace of sadness or worry for the future shows on her face. Her first battle of 2019 is over at one minute past midnight. It has been hard won, but as myself and Eamonn return to Cork the next day, we are not to know how short-lived will be its victory.

Just ten days later, I make the journey back to 108. Mum is very unwell with, I suspect, another kidney infection. In the early hours, Eileen and I call an ambulance and follow behind it to the hospital. There, over the next few hours, we find ourselves discussing painful realities with doctors. I am brought back to my beloved dad's demise, thirty-two years earlier, from motor neurone disease (MND): a time when unthinkable decisions had to be faced head on; a time when his courage never failed, despite the worst of circumstances. Now, as a new day dawns in the busy accident and emergency department, I entreat Dad to intervene. *She doesn't deserve this*, I whisper. *Help her.*

As Mum's condition continues to deteriorate, a doctor who seems no older than my eldest child suggests we consider a DNR order. Do Not

Resuscitate. The magnitude of this is hard to bear, yet as I absorb his words I have no doubt Mum would have only one request in such a scenario: *Bring me home.*

I know it is what we must do. By lunchtime, Eileen and Michael arrive to take over my shift, as do my two sisters. I drive back to 108 and, exhausted, let myself in to the quiet, empty hall, with only the dog to welcome me.

I sit for a while in the strange silence, scrolling through text messages and emails, when I see a name in my inbox that gives me a start. Johnny Watterson. My heart jumps as I put down the phone and close my eyes, the past crashing into my present.

Johnny was the journalist who, twenty-four years previously, had broken the explosive story in the *Sunday Tribune* that Irish swimming coach George Gibney had abused young swimmers in his care for over twenty years. Swimmers such as myself. As the fallout rained down in endless discussion and debate in the media, it almost broke my 28-year-old self. The impact of the events of that time lasted for many years. Just a year ago, my path had crossed with Johnny's once more, when he wrote a follow-up piece 25 years after Gibney was first charged, in 1993. When agreeing to be quoted in that article, using my own name for the first time, I had hoped I might finally see the end of the interest in our story. I must have been wrong.

What can he possibly want now? I wonder. I close the inbox without reading the email. Later will be time enough.

1

Number 108

Returning from the hospital that day, 108 had seemed empty, less like the home it had always been. Was Mum's presence the missing link without which our home would become soulless? A house without a heart? Could 108 feel Mum slipping away?

Some may think this foolish, believing a house to be just bricks and mortar, but I had grown up knowing differently as I listened to Mum and Dad's many tales of their first home in Killybegs,

County Donegal, the 'Little White House on the Hill'.

Returning to Donegal from London as a young couple, Mum and Dad had watched their house being built, brick by brick, and imagined it a palace when they moved in, the perfect home, where they could raise their two young daughters among the hills of Dad's childhood.

Just a few years later they had to make the difficult decision to relocate to Dublin when Dad was offered a 'good' job – leaving boatbuilding behind for management with Bord Iascaigh Mhara. Ahead of Mum and my sisters, Dad moved down to start the new job and find accommodation. During this time, he was desperately lonely without family or friends and every night, and often in the mornings too, he wrote home to his wife and girls in Donegal.

No one listening to those stories, or Mum reading some of those letters to us when we were young, could ever doubt that the Little White House on the Hill captured their hearts, but it was Dad's final letter before they cut ties with it forever that had really spoken to me of home from my earliest days. This was the letter we most frequently requested Mum to read.

Dearest Agnes,
Before I began to write this letter, I made a point of addressing the envelope, addressed to home, for never again will I write to you, to the same address. There is no need to go over all the happy memories, there is no writing pad big enough to write them all in. Soon, very soon, we will go, we will go as quickly and as quietly as we can. If houses had feelings, we would have to tip-toe out and close the door softly to save being heard ...

It would be a few more years before they would buy a house in Dublin, but when they did, they managed to once again create a special home in 108.

I could never remember the house being as

quiet as it was now, as if it was holding its breath. Entering the kitchen to make a cup of tea, my eyes were immediately drawn to Mum's empty chair in the centre of the room, her glasses and iPad beside it. This was the same spot where my grandfather had sat every day when he came to live with us, contentedly smoking one cigarette after another, the ashtray beside him overflowing. Before that it was where, on the rare days when as children we were too unwell to go to school, we would lie on an old comfy armchair covered by a blanket, as Mum filled the kitchen with the smell of dinner, brown bread and cakes as *The Gay Byrne Show* and *Dear Frankie* marked time on the radio.

Pained by the sight of her glasses and iPad, I moved into the sitting room, the largest room in the house with a big window running almost its full length, looking onto the front garden. As a child, I'd thought it to be enormous. A large couch and two chairs now took up most of it, the 'good table and chairs' for Sunday dinners and special occasions long since gotten rid of. A fireplace and sideboard sat at either end. I sank back onto the couch, drained by tiredness and sadness. Various photos of happier times were framed about the room. I lay my head against the back of the couch, wondering how Mum was doing. Above me, a large crack on the ceiling caught my eye. Despite my morose mood, I smiled.

'That was caused by yourselves and the McCartneys,' Mum used to say, referring to our Carlow cousins. 'You were wild when you got together, jumping off beds upstairs and running all over the place.'

I looked around the room. Mum's touch was everywhere. She'd a great eye for interiors, always keeping the décor up to date with the latest trends. Immaculate custom-made cream curtains ran the length of the window, perfectly matching the carpet and seating. Cushions scattered about the couch were updated regularly. I wondered as I looked around, what tales would this room tell? Along the length of the window was a

windowsill made of a rose-tinted, dark, polished
wood, wide enough for us to sit on. The same
wood was used on the mantelpiece and shelves
next to the fireplace, upon which sat numerous
photos. Each photo told its own story. However,
the story behind the shelves and the windowsill is
less obvious.

Years ago, when Dad was a young father and in
full health, his job involved occasionally travelling
to Norway to inspect trawlers which were being
purpose-built. At the time, our house was a work
in progress and with a young family of five,
money was tight. Furnishing the sitting room
was still one of the many jobs on Mum and Dad's
to-do list. However, on arriving home from one
particular Norwegian trip, Dad was very excited;
he had sourced a beautiful wood to make shelves
and a windowsill. With carpentry in his blood,
he had an enormous love for all things wood, and
this particular wood had captured his heart. This
was the 1960s, a time before large DIY shops, a
time when flat-pack furniture was non-existent

and variety in wood, zero. Mum was delighted at his news, not so much about the wood but the fact that work was finally to begin on the sitting room. Unfortunately, as the wood was to come from Norway there would be quite a wait.

Weeks later, the doorbell rang. A man told Mum he had a delivery for her. Behind him she could see a large truck with what looked like the trunks of three enormous trees on it. It would appear her shelves had arrived, just not the way Mum had imagined! Horrified, she phoned Dad in his office to tell him our driveway was now filled with three large tree trunks, but it was of course no great surprise to him. He arranged for them to be taken to the boatyard, where they were transformed into the polished, high-quality, rose-tinted wood they are today, still largely unscratched despite the best attempts of my eldest daughter, Aoife, to write on them with a coin as a six-year-old.

As the sights and sounds of the past continued to dance about me, my mood lifted. It was in this room I'd held my birthday parties as a child and where we had sat as a family watching *The Late Late Show* and *Glenroe*. It was here Eamonn and I had announced our engagement and where family gatherings had culminated in lively sing-songs well into the night. I sighed, warmed by my memories. 108 had indeed been a loud and happy place. I checked my watch; it was mid-afternoon. If I were to get some sleep before going back to the hospital, I'd better go for a proper lie down, in bed.

The stairs seemed steeper than usual as I climbed them to my old bedroom. Weary, I pulled the duvet over me, closed my eyes and lay in the half-light, hoping in vain that sleep would come. Despite my body's exhaustion, my brain was racing, ducking and diving from thoughts of the future, of Mum, and of Johnny's still unopened email that lay waiting for me.

2

Through the Looking Glass

Drunk on tiredness, I looked around the bedroom, its surroundings so familiar. This had been my room as a teenager. How many days had I sat on the bed pretending to study, the room a mess, with clothes discarded on the floor and books and schoolwork thrown everywhere? I smiled as I remembered coming home from school one afternoon, thrilled to discover that not only had

Mum cleaned my room, she had also bought me fresh curtains and a new duvet cover.

'I thought you might like it,' she'd said, delighted by my reaction.

I sighed. Whereas downstairs in the sitting room I'd remembered a past filled with love and happiness, within my bedroom the memories were of loneliness and despair, centred around dark years when my life was outwardly defined by swimming, my great passion, but inwardly by something infinitely darker and more insidious, a secret life I would carry within me for a long time.

It had not always been the case that swimming was my passion, in fact swimming and I had had a bumpy start. I'd attempted to learn the skill as a four-year-old, but it was not love at first sight. Each Saturday morning, my brother Michael and I were brim-full of bravery and excitement on our way to our lessons.

'I'm going to put my face down.'

'Well, I'm going to jump in.'

But once in the pool we clung like limpets to our instructors, begging them to please not let us go. The fact that the end of every lesson culminated in our group being marched to the deep end to be 'thrown in' did nothing to help our confidence. It was a most glorious day when Mum decided not to renew our lessons.

Being naturally athletic, the search began for a suitable sport to replace it. At seven, I tried Irish dancing, only to retire almost immediately when at my first Feis the judges failed to spot my talent. Gymnastics came next, and while I loved back-flipping around the place, it never quite captured my heart. So, at the ripe old age of eight, I gave swimming a second chance and joined Otter Swimming Club. There, an older, braver me quickly mastered the basics. Once I'd learned to swim, I couldn't get enough of it. Within the pool I felt alive and free. I loved the challenge of every set, and from my earliest days enjoyed pushing myself to my mental and physical limits.

In everything else in my life I was pretty haphazard, and in school I didn't exactly over-exert myself, but in the pool I sought perfection. As I matured as a swimmer I never missed a turn, streamlined off every wall and no matter how exhausted I was, rarely ever skipped a length. What I lacked in height I made up for in determination, perfecting the most efficient dive and fastest turns in an effort to give me an edge over my taller competitors.

My talent was quickly spotted, and I flourished.

Competing in my first gala at nine years of age, the thrill of the race was like nothing I'd ever experienced. As I stood on the podium to receive my medals, the acorn of my Olympic dream was planted, and I had every intention of seeing it through.

Swimming became an obsession, and a day without it was never as good as a day with it. Sore throats, coughs and colds were kept quiet for fear I'd be kept out of the pool, and despite early mornings and the time it took out of my parents' lives, they never said no.

St Patrick's Day, 1976, I woke in a state of excitement. I was ten! Tearing open my presents, I almost exploded as I unwrapped a pair of red, lycra, racer-back swimming togs – the togs 'real' swimmers wore. Running upstairs to my bedroom, I pulled them on, admiring myself in the full-length mirror. These were nothing like the saggy, nylon togs I wore every day, these were perfectly fitting, Olympic togs. Yes, Olympic togs, because printed beneath the small white maple leaf of Canada were the Olympic rings and the words 'Montreal 1976'. I might as well have been given an Olympic ticket.

If anyone had observed scrawny, undersized me standing in front of the mirror that morning, they may not have fancied my Olympic chances, but the eyes of a child can work magic grown-ups can only dream of. Standing, shoulders back, I smiled at the tall, lean Olympian looking out at me. With a nod to an imagined full balcony,

I waved at my parents and family as my name was called. Stepping forward, heart pounding, I readied myself for my first Olympic race. Not for one second did I believe that dream might not become a reality.

By the time I was twelve, Otter had become a club for leisure swimmers and more and more of us left it to join the newly formed Trojan Swimming Club, set up by leading swimming coach George Gibney. I had a loyalty to Otter and my coaches, Sean McGlynn and Jack Smith, but as I sat alone at galas, I envied the large Trojan team. One day, as I lined up to race, I was thrilled when the Trojan swimmers, encouraged by Gibney, began to chant my name and cheer me on. Onlookers must have smiled at their kindness, those from the big club cheering on the young, lone swimmer from Otter. My parents too no doubt were pleased at this recognition. As they signed me up to Trojan a few months later, they knew only of a charming, persuasive coach who saw raw talent in their daughter –

talent which, in his hands, could become that of a champion.

Initially, in Trojan I found all I was looking for. My friend Orla, who had introduced me to Otter Swimming Club, was a member and almost immediately I felt part of the team. Unlike in Otter, I had lots of fast swimmers to train against and became particularly friendly with a boy called Gary O'Toole. Although he was a year and a half younger than me, we shared a common rivalry, a passion for training and, above all, a will to win.

In my new club, Gibney lavished me with attention, correcting my stroke and feeding my Olympic dream with talk of going to the Junior European Championships and other goals. Each morning, I trained as part of a large team, in the pool at 5.15 a.m. sharp for a two-and-a-half-hour session, then back again in the evening for another hour and a half, sometimes with a short gym workout before it. Sunday was our only day off.

It wasn't long before this perfect spell at Trojan

ended, and its earliest signal – a harbinger of horrors to come – stands out in my memory.

I race home from school as usual, grab a quick bite to eat and am at the pool in time to gather with a few of my team-mates before our five o'clock session at Trojan. Compared to the mornings, when we are barely awake and say very little, the afternoon sessions are lively and fun as we chat between sets, splashing and joking. This afternoon's session is tough, and for the last fifteen minutes our coach George Gibney takes the breast-strokers to a side lane to do some work on their technique. I am among them.

Swimming is a highly technical sport and working on our strokes was often about making the smallest of changes, such as a quarter of an inch adjustment to the pitch of my hands or the very slightest delay to my kick.

Standing on the diving block at one end of the pool, my mind is focused on making the changes I've been working on. The others are now gathered at the far end and I am last to go. I take my marks and wait for Gibney's command to start ... but it doesn't come. I stand up, wondering if he's forgotten about me. He is standing on the deck close by, looking at me.

'What?' I ask.

He walks towards me and stands beside the block I am standing on, his face almost touching my body, chest high. I feel uncomfortable, self-conscious, puzzled. Have I done something wrong?

'I'm going to bed with you this weekend,' he says, and grins.

Before I have time to speak, he turns away, shouting, 'Ready, Go.' I dive in, my mind racing, all thoughts of my stroke banished. What did he say? Go to bed with me?

I speak of it to no one, and as the days pass

*and he says nothing else, I begin to wonder
if I've misheard him. Go to bed with me?
What did that even mean?*

*Within a couple of weeks I know exactly
what it means. I am thirteen years of age.*

Having given up on any hope of sleep, I rose
and crossed my old bedroom to stand in front of
the full-length mirror. I considered the woman
staring back at me. She looked tired. Old. I
leaned in, examining her more closely, trying to
see beyond the wrinkles and pale face. Could I see
her hidden scars? The healing? The victim? The
survivor? Could others?

I remembered an earlier time when I'd stood
in front of that same mirror, aged eighteen, as I
struggled to come to terms with the sixth-year
reference I'd got in the post that day from my
school principal. A school journey that had begun
with much promise six years earlier had gone awry.
At the start of secondary school I'd been a lively,

outgoing, confident child, who had blossomed fighting her corner in a big family. In school plays I was regularly the narrator, not because I was a good reader but because I was loud. Among my peers I was something of a leader, which I suppose is a kind way of saying I was bossy and liked to be the boss. Never short of a friend to call on, I'd had little difficulty making the switch from primary to secondary school. And in that first year life was fun, exactly as it should have been. But all that had changed with the onset of Gibney's abuse, and now my sixth-year reference described a girl my former self would not have recognised: *Patricia is a good worker in all subjects. She is a quiet, shy individual who appears to struggle to mix with fellow students.*

My face burned reading it, embarrassed at the timid, wary person the principal saw and furious for the strong, feisty girl he didn't know. But how could he have known? I was a person of many layers. What he saw was my outermost layer, but sheltered beneath that was my innermost self, who comforted me, told me I was great and assured me I could do anything. Without her in my life, I would have been a shell. But I knew deep down I was no shell, however I might have come across.

I was thirteen when I first began to add those outer layers. That was 1980, the year I stopped laughing. No one appeared to notice, not even myself after a while.

Those layers of defence weren't flimsy coverings, easily applied. They were cast iron, impenetrable, hiding inner me from the world, or was it the world from inner me? Beneath them I sang and danced, unheard and unseen, in the darkness. The protection they afforded me ensured that, five years into being sexually abused by George Gibney, I could look my eighteen-year-old self in the mirror every day and be content with what I saw. But what did others see? Was their view as narrow as my school principal's?

Disgusted, I put the reference into my cupboard, hiding it beneath a stack of books. Out of sight, out of mind. But it continued to call me throughout the day, and later that evening I pulled it out one more time and opened it. Despite only being hours old, it was already fragile, torn along a fold. Slowly, purposely, I tore it the rest of the way, then folded it over and tore it again and again until those words were ripped into the tiniest of pieces. They fell, scattering about the floor, some ink-side up. Words reduced to letters.

'You are not that person,' I whispered. 'Re-arrange those letters, make new words which tell the story of who you are.'

Now, as I gazed at my reflection, I felt compassion for that young woman, amazement at her resilience. And I wondered, had I fulfilled my promise to her?

3

The Past
Crashes In

I went back to the bedside and reached for my phone, and Johnny's message. It was a long email. After a polite introductory paragraph inquiring as to how I was, he informed me that a journalist called Mark Horgan and the media company Second Captains had been 'commissioned by BBC 5 Live to do an extensive series on the entire Gibney catastrophe'. What did that even mean? I wondered. The team were looking for input from myself and other victims. Would I be interested in talking to them? An email from Mark was enclosed, describing the intended podcast series.

As I read it, I noted Mark's tone and content were a perfect mix of compassion and explanation. I was intrigued, then a moment later dismissed my curiosity. Why would I entertain thoughts on George Gibney? Hadn't he already taken enough from my life, why would I allow him take even a minute of this precious time with Mum? But did I want to say a definite no? I decided to keep my options open and pinged off a quick reply to Johnny, letting him know Mum's condition and giving him permission to pass my email on to Mark, but making it clear that I would only give the request some thought if Mum improved.

Knowing sleep was futile, I decided to return to the hospital. I was in a hurry to see Mum again, wracked with guilt at having been away from her, even though it had only been a few hours. She was still in A&E. Despite having left her only a

short time ago, I was shocked at her appearance.
Lying on her back on the trolley, beneath a crisp
white sheet, she looked corpse-like. She didn't
stir when I arrived, exhausted from her marathon
fourteen-hour nausea session and fever. The urge
to disturb her, to prove she could be woken, was
difficult to resist. My sisters were not long gone
and, with my arrival, Michael and Eileen decided
to go home for a while too. Shortly after, a bed
on a ward was found for Mum and I was relieved
to see that with the hustle and bustle of moving,
she woke, alert and orientated. The following day,
even though she was obviously weak and pale, she
continued to improve, and I dared to go back to
Cork, believing we had dodged a bullet.

Arriving home, my feelings were a mixture
of delight to be back with Eamonn and the
children, and anxiety at being so far from Mum.
The following day our son Tiarnán was to be
conferred with a master's degree at the University
of Limerick. I was a ball of emotion as we set
off early that morning, relieved that Mum had

improved enough to allow me to attend, and tearful and proud of my son for all he had achieved. During the day we took lots of photos to send to Mum, who, Michael told me, had a card already signed for her grandson in her locker. I wasn't surprised. Mum never forgot an occasion.

On the journey home from Limerick the phone pinged with a text from Michael, and I paused before reading it, fearing its contents. Mum had had a bad day, sleeping most of it and disorientated at times. My heart sank. I knew things must be severe, as Michael would not have wanted to upset me on Tiarnán's graduation. What was I thinking, to have imagined she would recover so easily? Chatting with my brother later that evening, I decided I would return to Dublin the following morning.

'Will you be okay to go back up on your own?' Eamonn asked as he readied himself for work early the next day.

'I'll be fine,' I replied. 'If she is in any real danger, I'll call you.'

The long journey was not helped by major delays due to roadworks. As I drove, my thoughts were full of what-ifs. What if this is it? What if she never comes home? What will 108 be like without her? In between tears I tried to be hopeful, but it was difficult. I drove straight to the hospital. Michael was on his lunch break and already there.

Outside the ward I paused, taking deep breaths to try to supress the tears which threatened. I tried to picture the Mum I had left two days before, remembering how unwell she had looked in A&E, reminding myself not to expect the usual bright, smiling eyes I was so used to. I bit my tongue and wiped my tears before walking purposely towards her bed. If I had thought I was ready for whatever I might face, I was wrong.

Lying there asleep, Mum looked infinitely worse than I remembered. Her cheeks were hollow and sunken, her skin almost translucent. It was as if there was nothing between her and death except the spark of an inner spirit which was gently ebbing away. Shocked, I looked to

Michael, who had been watching for my reaction. He nodded. My brother and I had shared a lifetime of togetherness, so it was not surprising he could read my thoughts. I leaned forward and kissed Mum gently on the forehead.

'Hi, Mum,' I said, a forced cheeriness in my voice.

There was no reaction.

'Trish was at Tiarnán's graduation yesterday, Mum,' Michael said. 'Remember, you have a card here for her.'

She raised her eyebrows and nodded, but made no effort to open her eyes. I gestured towards the door and Michael followed me out.

'She's given up,' I said, unable to stop the tears, which flowed freely down my face.

'I know.'

'We have to take her home. Now, Mike, as soon as possible.'

'Yes, I agree.'

'I'll go talk to someone and arrange it,' I said, launching into full action mode.

Unfortunately, it was not as straightforward as that. The nurses looked at me as if I were crazy, but I was quietly determined and insisted that we knew what we were doing. Shaking their heads, they went off in search of a doctor to help us understand how ill-advised Mum's discharge would be. In the meantime, I returned to her bedside. She was awake.

'When am I going home?' she asked.

'We're waiting for a doctor so we can find out.'

She closed her eyes. 'I knew it,' she said, her voice barely a whisper, 'you don't want me home.'

My heart broke for her as no amount of explanation would convince her otherwise. She was weary and defeated and for the next hour or more kept her eyes closed and barely spoke. Finally, a doctor came, and we went out to the corridor to talk. He agreed that she seemed to have given up but was worried that we were not fully aware of her physical needs and that we would not manage at home. I assured him that I had nursing experience and that with her IV antibiotics finishing the next day there was no reason to keep her in. I could see he was unconvinced.

'When you look at her,' I said, 'I know you see a sick old lady, but she is so much more than that. She looked after her own parents, and over thirty years ago she nursed my dad at home as he died of motor neurone disease. In the end, he couldn't move any part of his body except his eyes. She made his dying at home possible; all we are asking is that if her time is running out, we give her the same chance. That is what she wants more than anything and she deserves that much.'

I could see in his face that I had hit home. 'I will organise an ambulance for tomorrow,' he said, holding out his hand to shake mine. 'Good luck.'

'Well?' said Mum, when I returned to her.

'Ambulance ordered for tomorrow,' I said, smiling.

'I'll believe it when I see it,' she said, unconvinced, and closed her eyes.

I didn't sleep well that night, worrying about

how we might manage if Mum's health was to decline further. Could we deliver on our promise to keep her at home? After all, I was no longer living in Dublin. Was I wrong to push it? Yet despite those worries, a large part of me felt giddy at the thought of her coming home, knowing the joy it would bring her. At nine the next morning Eileen and I arrived into the hospital, apprehensive about how we would find her. But what a vision met us! She was sitting up, perky as can be, hair brushed, lipstick and perfume on, and the widest smile on her face – a world away from the sick old lady I'd left the night before.

'Good morning,' she chirped.

We couldn't believe the turnaround. A young intern, who had been looking after her in the days before, arrived to sign her out and was clearly shocked when greeted warmly by her.

'I just can't believe it's the same person,' she said as we went out to the nurses' station to discuss Mum's medication and follow-up.

'I know,' I replied. 'Maybe in the years ahead

you will remember her, because that is what hope looks like. Yesterday she thought she would never again get home, today she knows she will.'

She nodded and smiled, still shaking her head as Mum gave her a warm goodbye and wished her well in her career.

Once we got Mum home she continued to thrive, eating well and slowly getting back on her feet with the aid of a walking frame, pushing herself more every day. I smiled when one day she asked if perhaps she should get a Fitbit to ensure she took enough steps every day. Hearing that, I knew it was definitely time to return to Cork.

On the drive home, my thoughts turned to Mark Horgan's email about the podcast. I'd barely given it a thought since the day I'd received it but now that Mum was on the mend, I wondered about making contact. But did I really want to tell the world my story?

Over the next few days I talked it over with Eamonn, our children and a few close friends, asking their opinion. As is his way, Eamonn listened attentively without trying to steer me one way or another. It was my decision. Friends were concerned and questioned what good it would do, worried that it might open old wounds. My now grown-up children, who knew about my past with Gibney, were more curious, wondering what sort of podcast was planned. I was torn.

In 1993, George Gibney had been set to stand trial for a series of sexual abuse offences, and had walked free on a point of law. His victims had never got their day in court. Then, with our co-operation, and without naming us, on 4 December 1994 the *Sunday Tribune* had told our stories, for the first time exposing Gibney by name in the Irish media.

As the fallout from those revelations raged, I remained anonymous, watching and listening from a distance, hiding, mortified and ashamed. Only Eamonn knew how broken it had made me, how hard it was to come back from. Now I had to ask myself: Was I still ashamed? Was I still broken? Did Gibney still have power over me?

There was only one way to find out. Before I could change my mind, I emailed Mark, and we agreed that he would come to Cork to meet me.

4

The Summer of 1981

One week later the doorbell rang, and I paused momentarily to take a deep breath before opening it to greet Mark. He had no idea the toll the morning's wait had taken on me. Anxious and on edge, I'd wondered what had possessed me to agree to meet a man I didn't know, alone in my kitchen.

'Are you sure you don't want me to come home and be with you?' Eamonn had asked before leaving for work earlier that morning.

'Not at all,' I'd replied, without a hint of the dread I was feeling, smiling and waving him off as if it were an ordinary day. But my racing heart told me it was anything but.

As I welcomed Mark into our home, we smiled broadly at one another. At thirteen years of age I'd taken smiles at face value. I'd believed in kindness, in caring and in love. By fourteen I'd learned not to be so foolish, that behind those smiles can lie an evil we can scarcely imagine, a darkness which others can't see. I learned to be wary and careful with my heart, and along the way I picked up a new skill, an ability to sense that darkness in a man, an instinct which would tell me, *Be careful of this one.*

As we walked to the kitchen, I had no idea if Mark would pass my 'test', but minutes later, sitting down at the table, my instinctive background check was complete. While I wasn't prepared to fully trust him, I knew I was comfortable in his presence. And with what we were intending to discuss, this was a huge relief.

Over the course of several hours, we spoke of his project at length. It was to be a series of podcasts featuring survivors of Gibney, recounting their stories and what had happened in the courts and afterwards. I questioned Mark as to his motive, somewhat puzzled as to why anyone would care about the story after all these years, let alone the BBC.

His passion for the project was obvious, and as the time passed I was surprised at how freely I spoke with him and how relaxed I felt in discussing things, off the record. When he left, instead of feeling exhausted and emotionally drained, I was on a high, delighted at how easy it had been. Surely, I thought, it was an indicator of how 'over' Gibney I was.

Later that night, after everyone had gone to bed, I sat watching television, a glass of wine in hand. As the evening had worn on, my feeling of euphoria had dissipated and I found myself slowly withdrawing from the family, distracted, as memories of the past rose up. I turned the

TV down, the canned laughter at odds with my sombre mood. My youngest child had not long gone to bed, departing with a goodnight kiss. Caoimhe was sixteen, carefree and happy. What a contrast to the secretive, closed and angry girl I'd been at her age.

Thoughts of another girl were to the fore of my mind also, one Mark had told me about that afternoon. She had met Gibney over ten years before I did, when she was only nine years old.

Prior to Mark's visit I'd only really thought about what had happened to *me*. I'd known there were other victims, I'd read their stories, but we had never had direct contact with each other. Now, as I sat in my sitting room that night, I felt connected to them for the first time. Somewhere out there was that nine-year-old girl, now grown up, who like me had had to pick up her life after Gibney, but she had lost even more of her childhood than I had. Tears began to fall and I let them go. I cried for that little girl, for myself and for all the other survivors of Gibney who had lost their childhoods, their innocence, their voices.

As I looked back on that teenage girl I once was, it was the loss of friendships which wounded me most, and one in particular: my training partner and companion Gary O'Toole. It happened during the summer of 1981 and it signalled not only a great loss in my life, but the time when Gibney's coercive control over me became complete. Although Gibney's grooming of me had begun soon after I joined Trojan, to be followed shortly after by episodes of abuse – events which at that time I could not have put into words – unbeknownst to Gary, his friendship had offered some protection from my abuser, as Gary and I were a tight unit, making it harder for Gibney to get me alone. Until the summer of '81, that was.

Gary and I were the best of friends, everyone knew it, and the sun seemed to shine every day that early summer as we walked the short journey to my home after morning training. Easy conversation flowed as we ran or dawdled along, his home too far away to travel from twice a day, much easier to stay at mine until evening.

Since my arrival into Trojan Swimming Club two years before, we had become a team of two: intensely competitive, bonded in friendship, oblivious to the transitions from childhood of developing bodies and changing voices.

Glorious hours between swim sessions were spent aimlessly wandering the estate where I lived or lying companionably in the sunshine, watching clouds race by as we spoke of the morning's training, hopes and dreams for the future and everything in between. Our relationship was uncomplicated. Were we boyfriend and girlfriend, people occasionally wondered? We didn't know nor care. We were soul mates.

As we looked forward to another summer together, we were unaware that storm clouds were gathering and life for both us was about to change forever. Gary was swimming exceptionally well and George Gibney had organised an invitation for him and another swimmer to train in the US, in California no less. No such invitation came my way. I would be without my friend for six weeks.

When I arrived at the pool for our final session together, Gary was waiting outside. His blond, tousled hair and enormous grin always lightened my heart.

Training that day was the same as ever, except for the knowledge that it would be our last session together for weeks. *This is what it will be like*, I thought, as I imagined not having him there to train against, chat to, or bitch with. As the two hours passed, I swam my heart out, racing from my thoughts as I feared what the future might hold without him being there. I had become wary around Gibney, conscious that he was staring at me, watching me, standing too close, fearful for when he might next try to get me alone. He'd spoken about Gary being away a few times, jokingly making comments about having me to himself. I'd laughed it off, but I sensed the danger, frightened for what was in store.

My parting from Gary that evening was

a slightly awkward affair, our respective lifts watching as we waved goodbye and promised to write each week. As we sat into our cars, neither of us knew what we were saying goodbye to, that the summer of 1981 would pass, taking with it our friendship and the carefree girl Gary knew.

Six weeks later Gary returned from the United States. Seeing him at the pool complex door, it hit me just how much I'd missed him. He was now a little taller, his hair surfer's blond from the Californian sun, his shoulders broader and his skin golden brown.

'Hi,' he shouted, and rushed to greet me.

Instinctively I pushed him away, wincing inside as I saw the flicker of hurt in his eyes. Nothing in my many letters that summer had led him to believe that anything had changed between us. Writing to him, I was free to pretend to be the girl he had known. In reality, everything had changed. I'd fooled myself into believing that things would go back to normal when Gary returned, that because of his very presence Gibney would back off. But as I saw Gibney's office curtain flicker, my heart sank, and a feeling of fear and dread swept through me. He was watching, just as I knew he would be.

With barely a smile or nod in Gary's direction, I opened the doors to the pool complex and stepped in. Gary followed, perhaps having missed my coolness, and once inside caught up with me. He beamed another 'Hi', caught my arm and pulled me back.

'I brought you a present,' he said, fishing in his gear bag and handing me a small packaged gift.

'Thanks,' I said, quickly stuffing it in my own bag, hoping Gibney had not seen, but a quick glance showed him standing at the end of the corridor, outside his office. He turned and went back in without a word. *Oh God, he's mad at me!*

I hurried away down the corridor and turned the corner towards the dressing rooms, passing Gibney's open door. *Please don't let him call me,* I prayed. Gary was following, chattering happily, oblivious to the drama he was witnessing. A cocktail of fear and dread churned in my stomach. I didn't need to see Gibney's face to know he was furious, at both the gift and the reunion.

Over the weeks that Gary was away, Gibney had increased his control over me enormously. He got me a job at the pool, so he knew where I was all day, and he policed my every move when I wasn't there, questioning me as to who I was with and what time I got home.

During that summer, I'd often babysit his young children. Within weeks of Gary's departure my connection with family and friends was reduced to a minimum, and in that controlled environment Gibney's abuse ramped up accordingly, the assaults more frequent and violent. With Gary's return I'd naively hoped that Gibney would back away, but I quickly realised there was to be no escape.

That evening's ninety-minute session was an eternity, with Gary chatting and joking beside me as he had always done, oblivious to my stony silence, or the fear I felt when he spoke to me as Gibney hovered above our lane, watching and listening, the warning on his face more powerful than words.

In the days that followed, Gibney orchestrated things at every turn to take me away from others, including my family. Walking with non-swimming friends, he would appear and offer me a lift, which I knew better than to refuse. He would insist I tell my parents not to come to galas, that he would bring me there and home. No one suspected it was all a ruse to drive me back to his empty office or to some lonely layby where he could rape or assault me. Sometimes I would protest, but more often I'd be silent, counting time until the attacks ended. He made it clear that my friendship with Gary was to cease. Occasionally I questioned this and even at times dared to converse with Gary, but Gibney's anger and jealous rages terrified me and within a short period of time I stopped resisting, becoming isolated, fearful, cautious and quiet.

Daily, I swam many miles, up and down the pool under Gibney's watchful gaze. Outside the pool, every conversation was monitored, every interaction noted. Many in the squad were still friendly and did their best to be kind and include me, but as my conversations were policed, my every smile monitored, it was a one-way street for the most part. From my lonely perch, I watched as one by one my team-mates forgot I was once fun to be around. Very occasionally, on days when I knew Gibney was elsewhere, I'd relax a little, chatting and laughing in the knowledge he couldn't see me, knowing this was how it could be … if only. However, such days only led to confusion among my team-mates, who were at a loss as to what to make of my unpredictable moods, as I inevitably retreated back into my shell once Gibney returned.

One such morning without Gibney stands out in my memory. My friendship with Gary was as good as over, and I was missing it dreadfully. Our session had ended, and for once neither Gary nor

I was rushing away. Gibney too had gone home, which was rare, and we found ourselves alone on the deck. We were standing within a few feet of each other and as the minutes ticked by, the silence in the deserted pool became filled with all we were not saying. Picking up our gear bags, we paused and looked at one another. For what seemed like forever, neither of us looked away. In that moment I was desperate to speak up, to tell him I was sorry, that I missed him, that I wanted to be his friend. Then he smiled at me, and as he did, I felt a stab of fear, wondering if Gibney was really gone. What if he walked in and saw us chatting? Quickly, I gathered my gear and left. As I entered the changing rooms, I didn't dare to look back as I softly whispered, 'Bye, Gary,' cursing my life as I went.

It was the final competition of that summer, the Irish National Championships, held in Cork. I was fifteen years old and swimming for the last time as a junior. This was what we had trained for all year, and despite what was happening to me, I was swimming out of my skin. Gary, however, was not. In happier times, only a few short months earlier, we had always celebrated our racing highs together and picked each other up after a low. But I was now avoiding him at all costs, and it was clear that day that he was missing the contact between us.

Walking to where our team were sitting in the viewing gallery, I suddenly spotted Gary coming towards me. In just a few short steps we'd meet head on. I knew he'd seen me. I instinctively glanced towards Gibney. As ever, he was watching. He stood up, his face like thunder, eyeballing me, before sitting down again and looking away. Such brief glances were enough to terrify me.

Gary couldn't see the look Gibney had given me, nor how shaken I was by the exchange. Neither he nor anyone else could know that I had been violently raped by Gibney in a toilet, less than an hour before. What Gary did see was me turning quickly to avoid him. I hurried away but he caught up with me, furious.

'Why are you being so mean?'

I looked him in the eye, willing him to see that something was wrong, but knowing that he couldn't. I can't recall what either of us said after that, but for me it marked the point of no return for our friendship. Barely coping with what Gibney had just done to me, Gary's reproach had cut deep, and I felt the final window of hope bang shut.

5

Captive in Plain Sight

When my parents signed me up to Trojan Swimming Club, they had no idea of the evil behind Gibney's interest in me. As a thirteen-year-old, who knew nothing but kindness and love, I was ill-equipped to understand what was happening as he insidiously dominated my thinking and isolated me from anyone who might come between us. The process of entrapment was quick, and in full view of my family and team-mates I became a prisoner – bullied, manipulated and abused, unnoticed by those close to me. So complete was Gibney's control of me that not only could I not see a way out, it didn't even occur to me to look for one.

During those years, I lived in a state of perpetual fear and anxiety. I became wary, watching out for his car parked up the road, on permanent alert in case he drove by while I was in company and caught me laughing. Cycling or walking alone, to or from the swimming pool or school, he'd stop to talk to me or pick me up, throwing my bike into the boot. If I were in company he'd pass, flashing a warning look in my direction to let me know he had seen me. So fearful was I of his disapproval, I often chose to walk home alone, despite the fact my team-mates were walking in the same direction. Even as I neared the safety of my home I was on edge in case he was waiting for me.

This was the 1980s, a time before mobile phones or instant messaging, but Gibney had his own way of keeping tabs. At any time of the day or night he'd call our house phone, cutting off after just one ring. This was supposed to be my cue to phone him back immediately, not an easy task as our stationary phone was in the hall, within earshot of everyone. It didn't matter if I was eating dinner with my family, doing homework or watching television, an immediate response was expected. Without one, the single rings continued, over and over. Some evenings, Mum would take the phone off the hook, and declare that she was contacting the phone company in the morning to have it checked out. When eventually, in a state of high anxiety, I'd manage to ring him back, whispering my apologies, I would be met with his spitting fury, warning me I'd better answer it the next time he rang, or insisting that he knew I'd been out, demanding I tell him where.

Sometimes, despite my reassurances that I was at home for the night, I'd hear his footsteps pacing outside my bedroom window, waiting to make sure I'd gone to bed. Closing the curtains, I never let on that I knew he was there, but climbing into bed on such nights I'd feel a mixture of despair and rage at my lot in life, and a loneliness that was hard to bear.

I yearned to be free. Sometimes I'd imagine what it might be like to chat openly with friends, to enjoy the camaraderie of my team-mates or to stand in the company of a boy, without fear. Occasionally, I dared to be that young, free, teenage girl I knew I should have been.

One afternoon, as the school bell rang, I ran to the bicycle shed, all fingers and thumbs as I wrestled with my bike's rusty combination lock. I was in a rush, daring to hope I'd not missed a certain, rather handsome young man from a neighbouring school whose journey home had coincided with mine the previous day. As I raced out the gate, sixteen years old, coat-tails flying, I rounded the corner and saw I was in luck.

'Hello,' he called, as I cycled past him.

'Hi,' I replied, jumping off my bike, conscious of my heart fluttering beneath my school jersey.

We ambled home together, a journey of less than twenty minutes, but what a thrilling one it was. Our conversation was easy, flecked with subtle flirtations. Along the way he seemed not to notice my anxious glances up and down the road, nor had he any idea that the absence of Gibney's car passing was giving him a rare glimpse of relaxed and happy me. Arriving home undiscovered, I was giddy. *He likes me,* I thought.

The following day I couldn't wait for school to end, and barely three minutes after four o'clock I once again pedalled out the school gates at speed. At times during the day I'd worried about Gibney seeing us. But the thought of chatting to Mr Charming made me brave and bold. Any warning voices in my head as I cycled out were drowned by the sound of my heart beating wildly, as I spotted Mr Charming dawdling along ahead of me. It felt good to be normal.

'Hi,' he said, as I hopped off my bike.

He was a little taller than me, wearing his school uniform and a gorgeous cheeky smile. We chatted easily, gently enquiring into each other's lives and laughing in that over-the-top *you're so funny* way you do when you are a teenager. We were sharing such a laugh at the very moment Gibney's car sped by, revving loudly. It turned the corner in front of us, tyres screeching, with barely a care for oncoming traffic.

'Wow, he's in a hurry,' said Mr Charming.

A stabbing pain hit my head and chest at the same time. *I'm dead*, I thought, imagining Gibney's car racing around the block.

'Sorry,' I said, jumping on my bike, 'I forgot, I told Mum I'd be home quickly after school. I'd better go.'

Without a backward glance I took off, desperate to get home before Gibney circled back but knowing I hadn't a chance. Minutes later, as I pedalled furiously up the hill, his car passed and dramatically pulled over in front of me. The avenue was deserted. I cycled up onto the pavement, stopping opposite his passenger door, well away from the car. I was less than three hundred metres from home. He put down the passenger window, leaned over and looked out at me. The heat of his rage hit me, his face close to purple, his lips pursed tight beneath his goatee beard. I no longer felt brave or bold.

'Who's your friend?' he said, in the quiet tone I feared most.

'He's not my friend. He's a friend of my brother's.'

'You two looked very cosy.'

'No,' I said, as if he were mistaken.

'What were you talking about?'

'Nothing.'

'Didn't look like nothing to me.'

I didn't reply but the silence was terrifying, like waiting for execution.

'Is that the first time you two met up?'

'Ye,' I said, kicking the front tyre of my bike, avoiding his gaze.

'Look at me,' he said, his rage bubbling closer to the surface. 'I'm asking you, is that the first time you've met him?'

'Yes,' I said, looking him directly in the eye, hoping I could out-stare him. Was his question a trap? Had he spotted us the day before?

In a flash, he was out of the car, slamming his door. Grabbing my bike, he opened the passenger door. 'Get in.'

As I stood motionless, watching him throw my bike in the boot, a voice inside me screamed, *RUN*, but I didn't. He gestured to the open passenger door as he walked to his own. 'I said … get in.'

The rest of what happened is a dim memory. I suspect it was no different to the many other times I enraged him. We would drive in silence, while inside my head I roared and screamed, calling him every name I could think of, venting my hatred and loathing for him, while another part of me sat, quiet and obedient, dreading what was to come. Eventually, we'd pull over somewhere secluded, where he'd interrogate me, his shouting less terrifying than his silence or his quiet questioning. I knew not to inflame the situation, always reassuring him I was telling the truth. Eventually he'd calm down, after which he'd sexually assault or rape me – as I counted time until it was over and he would deliver me home. Perhaps he got his thrills out of frightening me, or was punishing me for daring to cross him – and it certainly worked, as the trauma of the assault or rape was no more or less than that of the atmosphere he created on those drives, through anger or silence.

Arriving into the kitchen afterwards Mum would question me, curious as to where I had been, or cross that I was late. 'You always do exactly what you please,' she'd say.

Oh, the irony.

Invariably, later that evening the phone would give its usual one ring and the cycle would continue.

Such memories, even after so long, continue to evoke a sadness in me, especially when I think of my own girls. As I watched them grow into teenagers, I realised just how much of a child a thirteen-year-old truly is. My youngest, Caoimhe, still a teenager, enjoys life just as she should, and I think of the young girl I was, lonely and alone, despite living in such a busy, loving home. But it was that loving home which helped me survive those difficult years.

During that time, I lived in two very separate worlds: home, surrounded by the kindness, caring and love of my parents, Eileen and my brothers and sisters; and the darker world of abuse, in which I was controlled by Gibney. Although I could see no way of escaping his clutches, my home in 108 proved to be a refuge of sorts, somewhere I could catch my breath and be me, where for the most part I left fear at the front door. I always knew beyond doubt that I was loved there. Indeed, the memory of that love is all the more precious when I contrast it with the evil of Gibney, especially the love shown to me by the boys and men in my life: my two brothers, Ben and Michael and, of course, Dad, whose gentleness and kindness were ever-present.

6

The Seeds
of Happiness

When I look back on my life, it is in two distinct
parts: before and after. *Before* is when, for thirteen
years, I lived wild, free and innocent. Happiness
seeped into my soul, and among brothers and
sisters I learned to laugh and live life to the full.

After begins when my innocence was robbed
by Gibney.

In the *before* time, the links of love and

friendship were forged with a person to whom I've always had a precious bond: my younger brother Michael. When I recall those early years, I see him in every smile, every tear, every childhood row, every memory.

Michael and I were known as 'the wanes', a Donegal term for the 'wee ones'. The youngest two of five, we were always spoken of as one unit, in the same way twins might be. I was older by one year and nine months, a fact I never tired of reminding him, while he was at pains to point out that he was significantly taller and stronger.

As children, Michael and I were soul mates, sharing most of every day in our world of make-believe, adventure and games, with rules only we could understand. Of course, there were days when we fought, but mostly our rows were short-lived, as our desire to play together trumped our anger. Michael was the lovely child, the honest, genuine boy who wouldn't like to see anyone upset. I was a ducker and diver, a quick thinker, a chancer. Growing up in a large family,

I believed in talking my way out of trouble, with no conscience as to who else might get the blame. Sometimes, as I recall some of my memories of *before*, I feel sad, mourning the loss of that girl and the future she never had, but more often I smile as I remember her spirit and devil-may-care attitude to life. Something I had in spades one afternoon when an encounter with a fountain pen went terribly wrong.

I was about nine years old and shared a bedroom with my two teenage sisters and Eileen. It was a large room, upstairs at the front of the house. We slept in two double beds, buried beneath flannelette sheets and layers of blankets. Each bed was topped off by a light blue bedspread. Being so much younger, with few possessions of note, I left little impression on the room as its walls were covered with pop star posters torn by my sisters from *Jackie* and other such magazines. Dominating one corner of the room were built-in drawers and a large dressing table, made by Dad and littered with make-up bottles, hairbrushes, tweezers and make-up-soiled tissues. On quiet afternoons, while my sisters were at school and Eileen at work, I'd sit there lost in make-believe as I dolled myself up in front of its large mirror, not caring what trouble I'd be in if I were caught.

However, this particular afternoon that dressing table's contents were of no interest to me. I had my eye on a bigger prize ... my sister's fountain pen. Immediately upon entering the bedroom I'd spotted it, sitting there in its magnificence on her locker, its magnetic pull all the greater knowing how firmly she'd forbidden me from even touching it.

It was a thing of beauty. A slim pen with a smooth, ebony-black body, marbled with white and topped with a gold lid. I didn't dare touch it, but the longer I stood in adoration, the greater became the itch, until I could no longer resist. Stealthily, as if fearing I'd trigger an alarm, I reached for it, reverently rolling it through my fingers.

Its weight surprised me, so much heavier than

the pencil I was allowed at school. I pulled off the lid, its pop loud in the forbidden air. Beneath it was a slim, sleek, black neck, topped by a long, pointed, gold-coloured nib.

I touched the nib with my finger, pressing down gently, wondering if it were sharp. As I took my finger away the nib's indentation remained, marked by a tiny dot of blue ink. I tried to rub it off, but the blue stain lingered.

Sitting on my sister's side of the bed I held the fountain pen and wrote an imaginary note, looping my letters as grown-ups might. In front of me, my sister's school copy lay on the locker. I opened it on the middle pages. They were empty. Gripping the fountain pen as I would my pencil, I touched the sharp nib off the page, immediately lifting it off again as a large blue inky puddle appeared. I moved across to the other page, this time lightly touching it, as I wrote the letter 'e' over and over. With barely a line completed, the ink faded. The pen was empty.

Looking around I spotted, on the locker, an

ink-stained tissue upon which sat a glass bottle, barely two inches tall. Holding it to the window, I examined its dark inky contents. It was three quarters full.

If the fountain pen was forbidden, this bottle of ink was a mortal sin. I unscrewed the lid, releasing a wave of excitement into the room. Ink bottle in one hand and lid in the other, I clumsily shifted back slightly on the bed. The inky glass bottle tipped over, and in slow motion a single drop of dark blue ink escaped, splashing onto the pale blue bedspread. As though landing on blotting paper, the ink crept outwards in an ever-increasing circle, its colour fading like tie-dye as it spread. I stood spellbound. The stain was enormous.

I threw the pen on the locker and, hands shaking, replaced the lid on the bottle, returning it to its ink-blotted tissue as if it were red hot. Examining my guilty ink-stained hands, my stomach churned. I was dead.

Lifting the stained bedspread, I peeped underneath. Oh, sweet holy Jesus, the blanket was also an inky blue. There was nothing for it, I'd have to leave home. Tears stung as I wondered where I'd go. Raising my eyes to an imagined heaven, I clasped my hands in prayer.

'Dear Jesus, please help me,' I begged.

'Trish, where are you?'

From the hall downstairs Michael was calling. My naïve, gullible, younger brother, Michael.

'Thank you, Jesus,' I whispered, with a hurried sign of the cross, my escape plan already taking shape. With lightning speed I crumpled the stained bedspread and blanket into a heap, as if the bed were unmade, and stepped back. There was no sign of an ink stain.

'What are you doing?' said Michael, strolling into the bedroom.

'Nothing,' I said, sitting myself midway down the messy bed. Michael jumped up beside me, next to the locker.

'Look,' I said, reaching across him for the fountain pen. 'Caroline forgot to bring this to school.'

Michael's eyes widened.

'It's fab, isn't it?' I said. 'She lets me use it sometimes.' I was already sensing the itch in his fingers. 'Here, do you want to hold it?'

He put his hand out but quickly withdrew it.

'It's okay,' I smiled, 'it's out of ink.'

He took it and immediately set to writing an imaginary note, just as I had done minutes earlier. I lifted the messy ink bottle.

'This is the ink that goes into it,' I said.

Like a lamb to the slaughter he put the pen down and reached for the bottle, his hands turning a glorious blue as he touched its inky sides.

'Be very careful,' I said, 'if even a tiny drop gets on the bedspread it'll be ruined.'

Giddy with joy, I watched him reach for the pen and dip the nib into the ink. As he carelessly lifted it out, several drops dripped onto the crumpled bedspread.

'Oh my God,' I roared, jumping from the bed.

As if he were electrocuted, Michael leapt up,

discarding the fountain pen and glass bottle on the locker.

'Michael, what did you do?' I said.

He froze, looking from his ink-stained hands to the bed. Slowly I straightened out the crumpled bedspread and blanket, like a magician unveiling his trick, showing Michael the true magnitude of what 'he' had done.

Loud sobs filled the room as he stared at the enormous inky stain. 'Mum's going to kill me,' he wailed.

'It was an accident,' I whispered, placing my arm around him as we both stared at the ruined bedspread.

'But it's all ink,' he sobbed.

I turned him towards me, tilted my head to one side and in my most gentle, wise-older-sister voice said, 'Michael I think you should go downstairs and tell Mum straight away what you did.'

Tears spilled down his freckled face.

'Don't worry,' I said, hugging him close, 'I'll be with you.'

So down we went, me leading the way, every inch the kindly older sister, delirious with joy inside. I have no recollection of what Mum said, nor of the punishment, but I clearly recall going to bed later that night, minus a bedspread and blanket, feeling on top of the world.

It was years later before I told Michael the truth, and when I did he barely remembered it. He had plenty of his own memories of a childhood shared, of a friendship that would withstand the tests of time, and forever cast us as 'the wanes', a team of two, as much a part of each other's lives in the *after* time as we were before. Yet such was the secrecy, fear and shame I felt during my teenage years of abuse that, despite us being so intrinsically linked, I could not share with him my hurt or pain.

It is strange to think that there can be any gain from the most brutal of losses. Dad's early death cast us all onto an ocean of mourning, which we would each navigate for many years. Yet there have been times when I have been thankful that the disease that unsparingly took everything from him at least spared him one thing: knowledge of Gibney's abuse.

Dad's presence in my life was steadfastly positive, loving, giving, our relationship one of the most important to me. He was proud of all his children equally, and while he supported my drive to become a top-class swimmer, he never pushed me, more interested in how I behaved in defeat than in victory. There are many stories that illustrate Dad's nurturing influence in my life, but there is one that perhaps best exemplifies it.

Not long after my ninth birthday, I step out of the dressing rooms onto the deck of Glenalbyn pool to compete in my first gala. The deck is busy on both sides, with competing swimmers of all ages gathered beneath their club flags. The pool gallery too is full to capacity with parents and siblings, and I am a little overawed by the noise of their vociferous support. I sit with my team and thankfully don't have too long to wait for my first race. There's a fine line between excitement and terror and both emotions are present in abundance as I – skinny and undersized – walk towards the diving blocks.

Shaking slightly, I climb up on the blocks and take my marks, waiting for the starter's whistle, the butterflies out of control in my belly. Before I have time to think about the race ahead, the whistle blows and I take off. Diving into the cool water I leave all fear behind, relishing the sensation of adrenaline rushing through my body and my ferocious will to win. I swim my heart out, and when I finish ahead of my heat I feel an exhilaration I'd never before experienced. Like an alcoholic who will forever remember their first drink, I am hooked.

However, the pleasure of that race is quickly wiped from my mind at the thought of the next one, the one hundred metres butterfly. Of the four swimming strokes, butterfly is the one which demands the most strength and endurance, neither of which tiny nine-year-old me has much of.

Sitting in line, trembling, I wait for my heat, imagining my arms struggling to recover over the water, my head unable to lift clear to breathe. As each race starts I edge nearer the top of the line, and watch horrified as one young swimmer is pulled out of the water, sobbing, unable to finish her race. A steady trickle of tears fall down my face and my fear morphs into terror. Embarrassed, I keep my head down, the tears falling on my bare legs. There's no way I can finish three lengths butterfly! The heat before me take their marks. The whistle blows. They dive in. My race is next.

An official, dressed in white, walks

towards me and takes my hand. Like someone condemned to execution, I follow her to my lane as my fellow four competitors are shown to theirs. Standing beside the diving blocks I struggle with my goggles, as no sooner have I put them on than they steam up with the combination of tears and heat from my fear. For the third or fourth time I wipe them clean just as the referee blows his whistle. Reluctantly, I climb up on my starting block and look down the pool. It is a longer pool than the one I train in. My tears turn to loud sobs as I look to the far end. It's miles away.

'TAKE YOUR MARKS,' shouts the referee.

I step forward, my sobs rattling the length of my body as I wait for the dreaded whistle. Suddenly, a hand taps me on my back. I stand up and there beside me is Dad. From my spot on the starting blocks we are almost the same height.

'*Do you not want to swim?*' *he says.*

'*No,*' *I wail loudly, not caring who sees or hears me.*

Dad puts out his hands and scoops me up. Not even taking my goggles off, I wrap my arms around his neck, clasp my legs about his waist and bury my face in his chest as he carries me away. Passing rows of spectators, I keep my head down, my face burning in embarrassment. Inside, though, I am singing. Dad has saved me.

Looking back on that memory, I smiled as I imagined what I never saw: Dad vaulting the barrier to come on deck when he saw me upset, coming to save the day. He didn't care a jot about my winning or losing, or what lessons I might learn by trying and failing. His only concern was my happiness. It was always the case with Dad, and for that, I thank him to this day. Knowing the value of happiness meant that when I had to fight for it, in the *after* years, I was able to rise to the enormous challenges life had in store for me.

Mark was due to visit again in a few days to begin recording my interview for the podcast. Since our first meeting, I'd begun to get cold feet, wanting to cancel. But my memory of Dad renewed my courage. It was time to step out of the shadows, to speak out and let my voice be heard. Maybe somewhere, someone would hear my story and believe that if I could be happy again, so too could they.

7

Escape

By early March 2019, Mum was getting stronger every day, so much so that we dared to dream that our fears for her had been misplaced. Cautiously, we wondered what we might do for her eighty-eighth birthday at the end of the month, although we did this by text, afraid that to even whisper it aloud might tempt fate. Although still frail, she'd ventured out on a few occasions with Michael and Eileen to revisit some of her favourite haunts, such as Avoca and Kilquade Garden Centre, where her love of coffee and plants could be indulged. As I made my way to Dublin for my weekly visit, I hoped that I too might get a chance to take her out.

The following day I was more than surprised when Mum agreed to come for a spin in the car with me. She'd been quiet and withdrawn all morning, leaving me to wonder what might be occupying her mind.

'Will we go to Dad's grave?' I asked, as we drove down the road.

She didn't answer and, wondering if she had heard my question, I glanced in her direction, just in time to see her brush a tear from her cheek.

'Oh, Patricia, I'd love that.'

'I'm sure Dad's missed you,' I said, reaching over and squeezing her hand.

Of all the places Mum loved to visit, Dad's grave was top of the list. Since he had died in 1987 it had become a special place for her, where she could spend time with him and show her continuing love the only way left to her, by bringing fresh flowers and potting up containers with cheery-coloured violas, geraniums and cyclamen. Driving in the gates of the graveyard, we were greeted by masses of daffodils waving in the breeze as we passed.

'Aren't they beautiful?' Mum said, a cheeriness in her voice I'd not heard yet that day. As we parked a short distance from the grave there was a hush in the car and I sensed Mum's pleasure and pain.

'Come on,' I said, getting out and opening her door.

'I don't think so, Patricia. I can see it from here.'

'Aw, Mum, I've the wheelchair in the car, all you have to do is sit into it.'

She released her seatbelt with a sigh, which I took as a yes. I tightened her scarf around her, helped her out of the car and slowly pushed her along the very bumpy path towards Dad's grave. The wind was biting, but the sky was the most glorious blue with the sun doing its best to take the cold edge off the day.

'Oh, my goodness, it's lovely,' she said, as we stopped at the grave and she saw the filled pots and fresh flowers on it.

'Oh ye of little faith,' I laughed. 'I told you it was well looked after in your absence.'

We both fell silent for a moment, each lost in our own thoughts. The reality of being at Dad's grave, pushing my once vibrant mum in a wheelchair, was all too real. I couldn't hold back my tears, and as I tried to stop them falling, I glanced towards Mum. She was also crying. I bent towards her and we hugged, neither of us willing to share what we'd been thinking.

'I really know how to give you a good time,' I said, letting her go, and we laughed together.

The visit to the grave worked its magic. From a poor beginning, it ended up a lovely day. We skipped coffee in the small graveyard café and instead drove to Killiney Hill, a place Mum and Dad had brought us most Sunday afternoons as children. Sitting in the car park below the hill we reminisced on the many days we had climbed to the top to see the castle and obelisk, racing ahead of Mum and Dad, imagining all sorts of stories of ancient Ireland, before chasing each other down again.

From there we drove to Dalkey, with Mum chatting all the time, retelling stories from the past, most of which I'd heard many times before but the occasional one I'd not remembered. In Dalkey we stopped for a while and sat quietly looking out onto Dalkey Island, the clouds reflected in the unseasonably quiet and calm water. Returning home content after our couple of hours, neither of us thought for a minute that we had visited Dad's grave together for the last time.

The following day I drove home to Cork. In the car I had a lot of time to reflect on the day out with Mum. It had been wonderful, but over-riding all the memories was that moment at Dad's grave, when reality had dawned and it had hit me: that after thirty-two years the day was coming when it would no longer be known as 'Dad's grave'. It was hard to believe he had been gone so long, but despite the years, my memories of him were still so strong. As a child, Dad had been a giant in my life, and even though his final days battling MND had greatly diminished him physically, he remained my hero. Just as he had been one summer's day many years before, when a letter I received from him made a lifelong impact.

When I was sixteen I escaped for a month during summer to Marbella, Spain, where I worked as a babysitter for a family. I had met this family through swimming, and Gibney, knowing them, had endorsed my trip. In fact, he'd actively encouraged me to go. As I look back, I wonder at his motive. Was it that he had another victim at home, or had he wanted to ensure I had no contact with my fellow team-mates during that time? Whatever the reason, I was greatly looking forward to the experience and the time away from Gibney. I could barely remember ever having had such freedom.

Such was my desire to escape, it was only at

the airport, as I said goodbye to Mum, that the enormity of leaving my family hit me, but my sadness was short-lived. I was determined to make the most of this opportunity and I certainly did. The children were aged three to twelve and a pleasure to mind. Knowing Gibney was not going to appear around a corner, I was able to relax, to converse unguarded, to laugh freely, something I hadn't done for over three years. It was strange to be with a family, yet not part of it. Two other families were holidaying with us, one of which had teenagers, so I had lots of company. I thoroughly enjoyed the experience and during the month I rarely entertained a single thought of Gibney, but late at night I did miss my own siblings and even more so Mum, Dad and 'home'.

Two weeks into my holiday a letter arrived for me. I knew from the writing it was from Dad. This surprised me, as if anyone were to write I would have expected it to be Mum. I was sorely tempted to immediately rip open the envelope and read it but decided to wait until the evening so I could enjoy some precious time alone with

Dad when everyone was in bed. In the two weeks, I'd only phoned home twice. Now, with a letter in my possession that two weeks seemed like an eternity, as did the two more stretching out in front of me. During that day, as we enjoyed time on the beach and an evening eating out and strolling the town, I enjoyed many secret smiles as I thought about settling to bed later and opening my letter, looking forward to news from home and wondering what Dad had to say.

The evening dragged on a little but finally the children were tucked up for the night. I hurried to my bedroom, sat on the bed and pulled the letter out from where I'd left it under my pillow, pausing for a moment to savour it. It was a blue envelope, with my name and address written on it in Dad's familiar scrawl. I turned it over and opened it carefully, afraid I might damage the contents if I were to rip it. Inside was a letter and a second envelope. I pulled out the letter first. It had been folded into four perfect squares. Turning it over, I was disappointed to see it was only one page long. Stretching out on the bed, I propped myself up on my pillows and began to read.

Dear Patricia, it began.

Dad had a wonderful way with words and even in such a short letter I could feel his warmth and sincerity, as I read how he hoped I was happy. But it was only when I came to the end, where he spoke of the quietness in the house and how he missed me, that I understood why the letter was so short; he hadn't wanted to make me lonely. I smiled, brushing my tears away; he had failed in that! I read the one page over and over. Wallowing in my loneliness, I could almost hear his gentle voice next to me, soothing me. Then I remembered the other envelope inside the letter. I pulled it out. It had been folded in two and was sealed. On it, Dad had written,

Not to be opened until the night before you come home.

What! Was he serious? I felt a flash of impatience at the ridiculousness of the request, immediately toying with the idea of tearing it open. Did he really think I'd wait? However, a part of me felt I shouldn't open it. He had specifically asked me not to. He must have his reasons. I put it to one side, sorely tempted. While I was desperate to read whatever was inside it, I knew that once I did, I'd regret it. So I picked up the other letter once more and re-read it another few times, before carefully re-folding both and putting them back into the envelope. Lifting my pillow, I placed them underneath, drifting off to sleep, my thoughts filled with my family back home.

Over the next couple of weeks there were times when I felt very far from home, and greatly missed the noise and arguments of my own family. During such moments I would sneak back to my room, whenever it was possible, and reach beneath my pillow for that envelope. Holding it in my hands, turning it this way and that, I'd wonder what was written inside. But I resisted the temptation, which was most out of character for sixteen-year-old me, making do with reading Dad's other letter instead.

Finally, the last day of our holiday dawned and by that evening I could barely contain myself. It was officially *the night before I came home*. Sitting on my bed, I lifted my pillow and took out the still-sealed second envelope. With a slight tremor in both hands I carefully tore it open.

Inside was one large page, folded into four to fit in the envelope. Surprised and somewhat disappointed, I discovered that written on it wasn't the anticipated letter I'd imagined, but a poem. There was no title on the poem, but above it Dad had written,

Directions for your homecoming.

As I began to read, I heard Dad's voice in every word, his gentle lilt, his soft Donegal accent.

Come quietly, softly up the path,
The wind will know you as you pass.
The little flowers that star the grass,
will lift their sleepy heads again.

The shy, the furred, the feathered things,
these will not scurry from your feet,
there'll be no rush of startled wings,
for gentle are you, ever sweet.

Then quietly, softly ah, once more,
your foot upon the path.
A part of me asleep will wake,
your hand upon the door.

I still have that poem from Dad, the page it is written on now yellowed and torn. I can recite it off by heart, and no matter how often I've said it over the years it continues to evoke the strongest memories of Dad and all I loved so dearly about him.

8

Breaking
the Chain

The worst of times followed that Marbella summer, one day more difficult than the next. While abroad, I'd tasted freedom, connecting with the girl I should have been, and I deeply resented returning to my old life under Gibney's control. Yet I saw no way out. To an outsider looking in, I was excelling within my sport, thriving under Gibney's coaching. The previous year I'd swum in the National Championships, competing at both junior and senior level in individual and relay events, and won a total of ten gold medals. I was enjoying trips abroad as a member of the Irish team and had the Seoul Olympics firmly in sight.

Beneath the surface, though, I was barely staying above water. On many of those trips abroad with the Irish team, Gibney was the coach, watching my every move by day and never missing an opportunity to carry on his abuse, day or night. At home I did my best to avoid him, walking a different route instead of cycling, or hiding or running away if I saw his car, but whether it was in my mind or in stark reality, he was always there, lurking over my shoulder, waiting to attack.

The following year, having not been the most diligent of students, I didn't get the results I needed to pursue my chosen career as a nurse and, against the norm of the time, I repeated my Leaving Cert. In order to do so I had to go to one of the few schools which facilitated this, Newpark Comprehensive School, where the sports complex I swam in was situated, where Gibney worked.

Regularly I sat in class, ever watchful for his face looking in the small window in the door, praying a boy would not choose to sit beside me, terrified of Gibney's reaction. Somehow, despite such distractions, I got the results required and, filled with hope for a fresh future, I took my place as a student nurse in St Vincent's Hospital.

It was a year later, when I was in my second year of nursing, that I made the whimsical, last-minute decision to join five fellow student nurses on a two-week holiday to Cyprus, a decision which would change my life forever, for the better.

We were on our way to Belfast airport by bus when I first spotted Eamonn. The bus had left a little later than expected but stopped soon after departure, when two young men with suitcases, one of whom was on crutches, waved it down.

'Is this the bus to Belfast?' they asked, in what we Dubliners would call 'a thick country accent'.

My first thought of them both was: what a pair of eejits. Subsequently we discovered they had been watching the All-Ireland football final in a nearby pub and had misjudged the distance to the bus and the time it took Eamonn, on crutches, to get around while his brother dragged two cases. On our arrival at our resort in Cyprus hours later, I discovered we were staying in the same apartment complex.

Over the next few days we spotted the two brothers regularly; it was impossible not to, as they applied copious amounts of sunscreen to their whitest of white skin, while sitting in the shade! By about our fourth sighting, and following a few brief hellos, it's fair to say I could sense the beginnings of a spark for Eamonn. He was tall, with black hair and a cheeky grin, but it was his dark eyes that attracted and unsettled me most. As the girls and I began to spend a little more time with them, I felt giddy, flighty and even girly in his presence. Finding a place to sit by the pool became less about proximity to the water and more about being within sight of the brothers.

One night, a few days into our holiday, I feigned illness and stayed in the apartment, not wishing to go out with the group of men the girls were meeting. Close to eleven I heard a knock on the door and opened it to find Eamonn standing there. Doing my best to disguise my delight, I listened as he spluttered and stuttered, just about managing to ask if I'd like to join him and his brother Seamus for the evening. With unseemly haste I agreed, and minutes later found myself sitting behind Eamonn on a moped, zipping around the streets of Limassol, my heart racing as I placed my arms around his waist, uncomfortable at our closeness and relishing it in equal measure.

The three of us enjoyed a lovely couple of hours together before, late into the night, Seamus disappeared, leaving us alone. Ditching the moped, we walked along the promenade, so close that occasionally our hands brushed. I wondered if he could feel what I did. Did he hold his arm a little closer to mine hoping for another 'accidental' touch? Did he wish to hold my hand as much as I wished to hold his?

It was the early hours when we sat down on

the promenade wall, barely an inch between us, and looked out to sea. It was a beautiful, warm night, the moon reflecting in the water and the waves gently washing along the sand. Unnerved by how close we were to one another, I jabbered on, talking about anything that came to my mind. Finally, my conversation dried up and we sat for a moment in silence, my stomach doing somersaults. I turned to look at Eamonn and as I did, he leaned forward, and our lips touched.

As if scalded, I pulled away. The giddy feelings of a moment earlier had vanished, replaced by a rising nausea. I jumped from the wall and took off, shouting for Eamonn not to follow me. Turning the nearest corner, I leaned against the wall, heaving, convinced that evening's dinner was on its way back up. After a few minutes I knew it wasn't. Taking a few deep breaths, I straightened up, mortified as I remembered our kiss and my hasty escape. Walking sheepishly back around the corner, I saw Eamonn waiting for me.

'Are you okay?' he asked.

'Yes, I'm fine,' I said, giving off a definite, *don't come near me,* vibe. 'I just don't feel too well. I think we'd better go back.'

Very little was said on the journey home as I wondered why I had felt so sick. Could it have been my dinner? All I knew was that the thrill I'd felt earlier riding behind him on the moped was now a distant memory, and that I no longer wanted to feel Eamonn so close to me. What I didn't know was that Eamonn's kiss had sparked a hidden memory, the memory of another first kiss, of a forty-year-old man, a scratching beard, a poking tongue and a confused, shocked thirteen-year-old.

Following our disastrous episode on the promenade, I was relieved to discover that Eamonn had not been put off and we were soon spending a lot of time together, lazing by the beach or pool by day and, despite his being on crutches, clubbing by night. I was high on life, experiencing a freedom I could barely remember, freedom to go wherever I wanted with whomever

I wanted, but most of all freedom to laugh. However, these joyous feelings came hand in hand with anxiety and guilt, the undercurrent of fear deeply ingrained in me after six years of abuse, so even as I laughed, I never truly relaxed.

As the end of the first week approached, I was thrilled at the prospect of another seven glorious days and nights ahead. This was the way life should be.

'See you later,' I said to Eamonn and Seamus one evening, in high spirits as I headed back to the apartment to ready myself for another night out. Opening the door, I was met by high-pitched screeches from the five girls I was holidaying with.

'Trish, look what arrived for you!'

On the counter was an enormous bouquet of flowers. An ice-cold hand of fear grabbed me by the throat, squeezing the air out of me.

'Open the card.'

I didn't need to; I knew exactly who they were from. With a sense of dread, I opened the small envelope which had been delivered with the flowers.

'Don't enjoy your holiday too much. I miss you.'

How had he found me? As the girls gushed over the flowers, questioning me as to who my admirer was, I tapped the side of my nose.

'Can't tell you. But please don't tell Eamonn.'

They were disappointed, but when it became clear I was not going to tell them anything they let it drop, quickly distracted by the preparations for our night out. True to their word, they said nothing to Eamonn, but as we went from bars to night clubs that night I was on edge, seeing Gibney in every dark corner. I knew it was ridiculous, he couldn't have flown over, but a part of me feared he might have. Climbing into bed in the early hours of the morning, sleep was nowhere near. *How foolish had I been to believe I could escape? It was hopeless.*

After a restless night I woke early and immediately thought of the flowers. Going into the kitchen, I looked at them. How strange that something so beautiful could be so sinister. Eating breakfast, I sat with my back to them, but although they were out of sight, they were not out of mind. As the girls left for the beach, I hung back.

'I'll follow you down in a while,' I said.

Once they were gone, I picked up the flowers and shoved them into a plastic bag, breaking their stems and puncturing the bag, as if it were Gibney himself I was getting rid of. What a bastard! The holiday had given me a glimpse into a world I could not even have imagined a week before, one filled with excitement, joy and fun, devoid of fear, isolation and abuse. It had shown me the person I could be, the person I wanted to be. If only.

One week later, in the early hours of Sunday morning, we travelled by bus from Belfast airport to Dublin, on the final leg of our journey home. Sitting beside Eamonn, my head on his shoulder, I wished the journey would never end. I didn't know how I was going to get Gibney out of my life but as I looked at Eamonn's hand holding mine I knew I had found something special and the nearer we came to our separating, the more determined I became that no one was going to take that away from me.

9

Endings and Beginnings

In the beginning, I barely noticed the shake in Dad's perfectly measured lines, his occasional stumble, his weakened grip. Dad, who had begun his working life in a boatyard at sixteen, was only in his late forties, a man as skilful with a hammer and chisel as any great artist with a brush. Although he had left his tools behind to enter management – marking his move to Dublin and leaving behind his dream of raising his family in the Little White House on the Hill – the sawdust of the boatyard floor was never far from his shoes, a pencil always behind his ear.

At twenty, the second youngest of his brood, I determinedly ignored the obvious until one day, as I watched him struggle to screw a plug socket into the wall, I knew I couldn't continue to look away.

I don't remember the exact month when Dad's consultant summoned Mum for a meeting. As a student nurse I was the obvious choice to accompany her. Dad had been admitted to St Vincent's, my teaching hospital, for 'tests'. Earlier that morning I'd sat by his bedside and he'd told me he hoped it was a brain tumour.

'At least they'll be able to treat it,' he said.

The ward was awash with secrets that day. I hadn't told Dad of our planned meeting with the consultant, and my fellow nurses were in hiding, already aware of the diagnosis.

'It's motor neurone disease,' the consultant

said. 'I'm sorry, there's no treatment and no cure.'

Mum and I sat waiting for the explanation. What was motor neurone disease? The consultant rambled on, but I didn't hear a word. It was his body language I was tuned into, the pity in his eyes, the tilt of his head, the tone of his voice, all telling us there was no hope. I stumbled out of his office a short time later like an over-wound clock. That was the first of the killer conversations. There were many more.

In less than one year, MND was on a winning streak. Initially, we'd marked Dad's losses from month to month, as his hands became weaker or he stumbled occasionally, but all too soon the deterioration was noticeable week to week, as his stumbles turned into falls. Even the most basic of tasks proved difficult. During this time, Dad clung to two things: his love for Mum and the family, and his trademark sense of humour, which he and Mum shared.

From my earliest days I remember him speaking

excitedly of his plans to take early retirement. He would build a house in Killybegs, County Donegal, a holiday home for the whole family to enjoy, not far from the Little White House on the Hill. MND stole those dreams from us all. Dad did indeed get the early retirement he'd wished for but not the future he'd dreamed of.

I can only imagine his final day at work. Knowing Dad, I suspect he spent it carefully noting every detail of the day, pausing before leaving his desk for the last time and smiling as he said goodbye to friends and colleagues. On his return home later that evening I quizzed him, wondering had it been as hard as I'd imagined.

'Trish,' he laughed, his trademark humour intact, 'I'm the first man to fall on my way in the door to my goodbye drinks, instead of on my way out.'

Within a few months, there were more goodbyes – to his much-loved tools, to driving, and to walking. It was impossibly difficult to watch his bravery as he faced each loss, and even harder to witness the times his bravery slipped. But of all these hardships, saying goodbye to his voice was the most difficult.

If I close my eyes, even after so many years, I can still hear Dad's gentle tone and soft Donegal lilt as he sings 'The Green Glens of Antrim'. A little less clearly, I can hear him comforting and soothing me as a teenager. He had enormous wisdom and taught me many lessons. At work he was known for his common-sense advice and at home he approached problems logically, almost always with a list of pros and cons. While Mum and I clashed on many occasions, our quick tempers culminating in raised voices and my storming off, slamming every door I passed, such was not Dad's style. I recall him all too often returning from work of an evening to find me in my room, furious at Mum over something and nothing. Barely giving him time to enter, I'd spew the ins and outs of my fury as he sat on the bed listening, nodding, and appearing to fully agree with my every word.

'So, will you come on down now?' he'd say, when I finally drew breath.

'No.'

'For me?'

'No.'

'Ah do, Trish. Come on down.'

It shouldn't have worked, but there was something in his voice and gentle manner which never failed to quieten me, and despite my anger and protestations I would do as he asked.

However, as MND took over, his days of coming upstairs ended. Instead, I came to him as he lay in bed or sat in the sunroom, a captive audience. I filled him in on all that was important in my life: the minute details of my latest visit to Eamonn or the ups and downs of my day on the ward. I took on board any advice offered and greatly enjoyed our chats. However, I was not deaf to the alarms ringing in my head, as his speech became more slurred and his body began to shut down. I just chose to ignore them. Until one day that became impossible.

While MND raced through Dad's body, it chose to linger about his chest, slowly paralysing his lungs. We grew accustomed to his wheezing and the rattling sounds within his chest, but the arrival of a new, high-pitched, whistling sound as he took a breath in alarmed us greatly. It was particularly frightening for Mum, as she listened to it in the loneliness of the night, fearing he might stop breathing.

'John's vocal chords are becoming paralysed,' the consultant explained. 'He will need a tracheostomy. We will make an opening in his neck, below the vocal chords, and insert a tube into his windpipe so he can breathe more easily.'

Up to this point I had believed the worst thing I would ever hear was that same consultant telling us there was 'no treatment, no cure'. I was wrong. Perhaps Mum and Dad were relieved as they listened, glad something could be done, but I was shattered, fully understanding what this would mean. Dad would never again sound the same and we were but a short step away from losing his conversation in our lives forever. It was too soon. I wasn't ready.

I was working the evening before his operation, so it was well after visiting hours when I finished my shift and walked the long corridor to his ward. He was sitting up in bed, bedecked in fancy wine-coloured pyjamas. He looked fragile and many years older than his fifty-four years. His face lit up when he saw me and I smiled back, walking towards him and determined to be brave. We hugged, but as he held me close I crumbled, crying softly as he comforted me as any dad would.

I finally let go, pulling up a chair beside his bed. We talked for a while, sharing titbits of our day until we could no longer avoid tomorrow. Dad was relaxed and somewhat relieved to be having the operation, and already looking forward to going home. I stayed as long as I could, relishing every word spoken, trying to remind myself what this operation would give to Dad, not what it would take away. Eventually, as the lights on the ward were turned out, I knew I could delay our goodbye no longer. We both knew it. Drawing on every ounce of strength I had, I stood up, holding his hand.

'Okay, Dad, I'm off.'

He nodded, giving my hand a little squeeze. 'See you tomorrow.'

'The very best of luck,' I said, leaning down and kissing his head. 'I'll be thinking of you.'

He said something, but his speech slurred so I didn't understand him.

'I'll have to lay off the drink,' he laughed.

With that, the tension broke. We shared a final kiss and I squeezed his hand an unspoken *I love you*, before walking away, each of us as brave as the other. At the door I turned and waved a final, cheery goodbye, but as I walked down the deserted corridor back to the nurses' home the crushing, burning pain in my chest was almost unbearable. An avalanche of tears welled up inside me, a cocktail of grief and anger ready to explode. *This is so unfair.* A loud sob escaped, and as it did, others quickly followed. In the solitude of the dimly lit corridor I slumped to the floor, my back against the wall, hugging my knees, keening as I rocked back and forth, my grief echoing around me until I was empty. My head was pounding as I cautiously looked up, remembering where I was. A pair of legs stood in front of me. Slowly I followed them upwards, past the white coat and up to the face looking down at me. It was an intern I worked with, who coincidentally was also called Eamonn. He was aware of Dad's diagnosis, as were others in the hospital, as a diagnosis of MND was a rarity in 1987. He held out his hand to help me up and I took it, mortified as I reached for a sodden tissue in my pocket, which had little effect on my streaming nose.

'I'm so sorry about your dad,' he said, his northern accent hitting me hard.

'Thank you.'

'Are you okay?'

'Yes, I'm fine,' I replied, walking as fast as I could down the corridor.

Gentleman that he was, he walked beside me

all the way to the door of the nurses' home. As I lay in bed later thinking of Dad, I had no more tears to shed. As with so much of what was going on in my life at that time, I kept the pain of that evening to myself, but despite my 'I'm okay, you can leave me alone' attitude, I was grateful to my doctor friend for his kindness, and as I fell asleep felt a little less alone.

Dad was only in hospital for a few days, and the 'trachy' was soon just another thing we all had to adjust to as we learned to care for it, cleaning it twice a day and changing it regularly. There was an inner tube that fitted into it, which we called his talking tube. While it was in place he could speak – not like before, but at least it was something. With this major intervention, Dad knew time was against him and he was desperate to sort out his affairs. He worried that Mum was not listening to how ill he was, while she despaired at him talking of a life without him in it. Such was her unwillingness to imagine such a life, that on occasion we would enter his room and he would lift a shaking hand to point to his trachy, which was minus the talking tube.

'Oh dear! Did Mum silence you?' we'd say, joining in his laughter, although sometimes his laughter would turn to tears, as would ours as we recognised his desperation, his need to make plans, while equally understanding Mum's pain.

During those dark days, Eamonn brought me sunshine. As I boarded the train for Cork, to visit him, I'd feel myself relax. Every mile I travelled was a mile further from Gibney – whose stalking continued – and from the heartbreak of home.

Eamonn lived in a very different world. Although he worked in Cork city, his family home was Ballydesmond, a small village in the north of the county, where they owned a shop. From the beginning his family had been more than welcoming to this Dublin girl, and I loved to visit. But there was one major drawback: I hadn't a clue what they were saying.

I had been exposed to many accents while
working in the hospital and holidaying in
Donegal, but nothing prepared me for the
wonder that is the Cork/Kerry blend and the
speed at which it is spoken. It was like arriving in
a foreign country where no one spoke English. I
should, of course, have instantly confessed that I
had no idea what they were saying, but I didn't;
instead I smiled a ridiculous amount, did a lot
of nodding and pretended I'd not heard them.
Unfortunately, the fact they owned a shop meant
there was more than just the family to contend
with. Not anticipating any problems, on one of
my early visits I agreed to help in the busy half
hour after mass. Unfortunately, someone made
the fatal error of putting me on a till. I'm not
sure if it was my ineptitude or the desire of most
of the villagers to check out 'Eamonn's girl from
Dublin', but the queue at my till was soon akin to
a Christmas shopping crowd. Coupled with the
fact that I had very little idea what anyone said, I
was somewhat traumatised by the time the shop

cleared. However, such episodes were a wonderful contrast to my everyday life, and once back in Dublin I got great mileage out of recalling them to family and to Dad, bringing a much-needed injection of laughter into all our lives.

Telling those stories allowed me to believe I was just your average girl, with a lovely boyfriend, living life to the full. And although the truth was unimaginably different, something really *was* changing within me. I had tasted freedom, and slowly, determinedly, my strength was gathering. Gibney's reign of terror was almost over – even if it brought with it an end to my Olympic dream.

10

Fighting Back

Life as a student nurse was busy, and there were no allowances for an Olympic hopeful with a full-on training schedule. Nights on duty were followed by mornings in the pool, and with Dad's deteriorating health it was becoming clear to me that something would have to give. In the end, the decision to walk away from swimming was an easy one.

Swimming, for me, had always been separate

to Gibney, even if it necessarily involved him. In the pool I was complete, whole, in control, my end goal unchanged from when I was ten years old. However, since beginning my nursing training I had not been performing well, but I had one more chance to make the Olympic training squad, at a 'home' gala in Belfast. Unable to get time off work, I finished a busy night shift at 7.30 a.m. and boarded the train to Belfast, arriving at the pool just in time for the afternoon session. Despite my lack of sleep, I was psyched and ready to give it my all. And I did, but this time it was not enough. I was gutted to discover I'd missed out by the tiniest of margins.

'I hope you enjoyed that last breath,' Gibney hissed as I emerged from the pool, referring to the breath I took one stroke before the finish, 'because it cost you the Olympics.'

I gave him a hard stare. *Fuck you, Gibney.*

And that was it, an invisible line crossed, the breakaway I had longed for finally secured. I would return from Belfast intent on leaving

Gibney behind, for good, even if it meant leaving swimming behind too. For ten years I'd worked for a dream that was now over, but instead of feeling crushed with disappointment, I felt liberated, and determined on a better future.

I immediately stopped swimming, and as a result became less predictable in my daily routine. Afraid of Gibney's reaction to discovering Eamonn was in my life, I travelled to Cork as often as possible rather than have Eamonn come to Dublin, but I was only postponing the inevitable. Soon, unbeknownst to Eamonn, Gibney became a part of most of our Dublin dates, either in person, lurking in the background, or in my head, as I feared and imagined he was near.

Perhaps Eamonn thought it was love as I squeezed his hand tight, not noticing the car which had pulled in behind us, or maybe that I was a little odd when I changed my mind about bowling after we had paid for our game, having spotted Gibney in the building. So deeply entrenched was my secret that I never thought to tell Eamonn that we were being watched or followed. However, alone with my thoughts, most particularly at night, I feared what the future might hold. Yet I had no intention of giving up Eamonn. *Let Gibney do his worst.*

As Gibney found it increasingly difficult to track me down, he changed tack, targeting me within the grounds of the hospital car park instead.

One afternoon, having finished a morning shift, I stood at the door of the main hospital with some co-workers. To any outsider watching, we were a gathering of young nurses, lively and loud, happy to be finished our shift with much of the day ahead. No one would have noticed my falling out of step as I paused to quickly scan the cars parked near mine, or my re-joining the chat as we walked across the car park, relieved there was no sign of him. Nearing my bright red Fiat Panda, I shouted my goodbyes. As I put the key in the car door my mind shifted to thoughts of Dad, part of me wanting to rush home to him, while another part resented having to. It was as I opened the door that I sensed he was near. It was too late.

'Hi,' he said, stepping in front of me and putting his hand on the door, his goatee-bearded face inches from mine.

I froze, but within seconds a hot flush of anger crept through me. Anger at his hand on my door. Anger that he was in the car park. Anger that he'd frightened me.

'I've to go home to Dad,' I said, surprised at the strength in my voice.

He didn't move, just stood staring at me. I held my nerve and met his stare.

Taking his hand from the door, he touched my cheek. Trapped between him and the car, I flinched.

'I like your eyes,' he said, his finger tracing the outline of the blue eyeliner I was wearing. 'You never did your eyes like that for me.'

'Get out of my way, George.'

'Why? Are you going home to your boyfriend?' he mocked.

'Let … go … of … my … door,' I shouted.

Surprisingly, he did.

I opened it and quickly sat in, but as I attempted to close the door he pulled it open and leaned into the car, his face so close I could count every hair on his beard, the smell of his breath, body odour and aftershave filling the space between us.

'Actually,' he said, standing back, smirking, 'I think your eyes made up like that make you look cheap … like a whore.'

I slammed the door and turned the key. Shaking, I reversed, without looking in his direction, his hurtful words echoing around the car. That quiet voice he'd used, I knew well. It was him at his most dangerous. However, this time I'd seen something I'd never seen before, a look of hatred on his face, the memory of which was terrifying.

In the weeks afterwards he seemed to care less that I might see him and often parked close to my car or stood beside it. Then one day he went a step further and entered the hospital.

I'd been nursing close to two years and within the hospital walls I dared to be me, chatting and interacting with my fellow nurses, doctors and patients in a world without the fear of Gibney. This afternoon had been a busy one, when I noticed a figure at the end of the corridor. A sharp pain shot up my arm to my neck as I caught a glimpse of a man ducking around the corner. Many people came and went around that corner every day, but for some reason this one had caught my eye. *Was it him?* I had to know. All sights and sounds of the ward disappeared as I walked in that direction, the rush of blood around my body loudly whooshing in my ears. The closer I got, the faster I walked, determined to find out if it was him. At the corner I didn't hesitate, stepping out, ready to confront him … but he wasn't there. I stood for a moment, scanning the group of visitors in front of me waiting for the lift to arrive, before opening the door to the stairwell. Pumped with adrenaline, I looked up and down the stairs, but there was no sign of him.

Turning, I walked back into the ward, my body still on high alert. *Maybe I'd been mistaken?* But as the hours passed, I was certain I had not been wrong. For the remainder of my shift I was on edge, hesitating as I emerged from behind a patient's curtain, wondering if he was on the other side and imagining he was waiting for me in every room I entered. Walking to my car that night I was more frightened than usual, but he was nowhere to be seen.

For the next few days I tried to convince myself I'd been mistaken, but soon afterwards he admitted it. He did so casually one day, as I walked along a path near my home, his car trailing beside me. He had been visiting someone, he told me, but when I questioned him as to who, he only smiled. I despaired. My final sanctuary had been violated.

I tried not to let my fears take over, but it was difficult. In the next few weeks he returned to the ward a few more times, walking brazenly up the corridor during visiting hours or asking a question at the nurses' station. It was strange behaviour, as even when I did see him, we ignored one another. However, with each encounter my fear rose that perhaps he was becoming seriously unwell and if so, what might he do? I didn't have to wonder for long.

He was sitting in his car, not far from mine, as I was leaving one day after a morning shift. Cursing him, I changed direction, returning to the hospital and taking the underground tunnel to my room in the nurses' home, a room I'd kept on so I could sleep better when on night duty. This room was on the eighth floor, which gave me an excellent view of his car. I'd told Mum I'd be home early, so waiting for him to leave wasn't an option, I'd have to take the bus. I changed into what I hoped were my least conspicuous clothes and went downstairs. As there was no back door to the nurses' home, I left via the front, with my head down, praying he was watching the main hospital entrance, which was in the opposite direction. Once out of the car park I ran across the road to the bus stop opposite the hospital.

There were a few other people waiting. *Perhaps a bus was due shortly?* I stood at the back of the bus stop and kept my head down, hoping that even if he did pass, he might not see me. I was wrong.

As the car stopped, I knew it was him without even looking up. He beeped.

'Trish,' he shouted, all smiles to the witnessing public, 'get in.'

'No, it's okay,' I said, not moving forward. 'The bus will be here in a minute.'

'Don't be silly. Hop in,' he said, pushing the passenger door wide open.

The voices in my head screamed no but, embarrassed to be part of a scene at the bus stop, I walked past my fellow commuters to the car and sat in. Immediately, I regretted it.

Neither of us spoke. It had been over a year since I had sat in his car, but the memories it triggered were intense. I glanced across at him, but he was staring ahead. His bearded face and the smell of his aftershave made my stomach churn. I tried to remain calm, but I was furious with myself for getting into the car. *What had I been thinking! Why had I not told someone I was afraid?* I knew without asking that he had no intention of bringing me home. He drove at speed, passing the places I had thought he might stop until finally we turned off the dual carriageway towards Enniskerry. *Oh my God, he is taking me to the mountains.*

'I thought we might go somewhere quiet for a chat,' he said, as the road became narrower.

'I've to get home. Mum's expecting me,' I replied, but he ignored me.

Not wanting to antagonise him, I said no more, but every nerve was primed. *What was he going to do?* It had been so long since he'd laid a finger on me, I was now more frightened than when I had been a child. Finally, we pulled into a car park by a wood. There were a couple of cars around, but no people. He took off his seatbelt and turned to me, smiling.

'So, how are you?'

'I need to get home.'

'I just wanted a chat. I've missed you.'

The sound of the door locking almost stopped my heart. He leaned across and tried to kiss me.

'Get off,' I roared, as he pushed himself towards me.

He continued, but something inside me flipped. A part of me had feared this moment for some time but suddenly I felt enraged. I roared and hit him like someone possessed. He recoiled but I continued, my pent-up rage unstoppable. Finally, he pushed me away and started the car, driving off like a getaway driver. Try as I might over the years, I have never been able to fully piece together the remainder of that afternoon. Did I get out of the car in the woods or did he drive off with me in the car? How did I get home? What I do remember clearly is the intense fear I felt and the conviction that he intended to kill me, followed by my clear belief, as I fought him off, that it was me who was going to kill him.

That was the last time George Gibney assaulted me. Despite being shocked by the events of the day I knew it was over, and I suspect, having witnessed my fighting back, so did he. Although he continued to stalk me, it was not on the same scale as before and even though I remained vigilant, I was less fearful. I also had greater worries.

Dad was dying. We all knew it, but no one wanted to talk about it. In the months after he got his tracheostomy, motor neurone disease took everything: his hands, so he had to be fed; his legs, so he had to be pushed in a wheelchair; his bladder, so he needed an indwelling catheter; and his voice, which became croaky and almost impossible to decipher. But it didn't affect his eyes. They continued to look at us, to plead with us, to laugh with us. As he lay in his special bed which rotated, we became experts in engaging in conversations without words. In the twilight zone between Dad living and dying, time seemed to slow down, as we cherished the tick of every minute, of every hour, of every day. Until we were down to our final week.

You'd think I'd have known, but I didn't. I

reasoned that he had a chest infection and was tired. Weren't we all?

'I'll sleep here tonight,' I said to my exhausted mum, and for the first time in eighteen months she left him.

As the family kissed Dad goodnight and went their separate ways, I turned out the lights, except for a small, dim one over the head of Mum's bed. Dad lay opposite, strapped into a large rota rest bed, which lived up to its name by rotating slowly from left to right, its motor a steady hum, mingling with the sounds of thick secretions bubbling and rattling within his lungs. As his bed turned him slowly towards me, his every breath was a short, frantic gasp. I watched his chest rise and fall so rapidly I wondered how any air had time to enter or exit.

'I'll suction you, Dad,' I said, turning off his bed. Suctioning Dad meant passing a long thin tube down his tracheostomy tube and switching on the suction machine, which sucked the secretions out in an alarmingly noisy way. It was a task I'd grown used to as a nurse, detaching myself from the patient as I passed the suction tube down their throat. I'd learned to ignore the fear in their faces as they gasped, unable to breathe, while the tube removed the thick secretions blocking their air passages. It was a simple choice: do this or let them drown.

But that night, as I passed the tube down Dad's 'trachy' and watched his body gasp for air, I felt cruel beyond measure. Finishing as quickly as I could, I bent down, putting my arms around him, resting my cheek against his, my apology unspoken as his warm tears mixed with mine – the closest to a hug this disease would allow. There was an agony within me, a mixed potion of fury and sorrow, keening and screaming beneath the surface.

After a few minutes I stood, wiping both our tears, and reached for his night-time tablets from the well-stocked locker beside his bed. I tipped out two into a small container. Another ten or twelve tumbled after, the tiny white tablets covering the bottom of the measure. A lethal dose.

In the half-light I looked at Dad's skeletal, contorted body. The gaoler of his active mind. *Was waiting to die, living?*

Holding the measure of tablets in my hand, I imagined tipping them into his mouth. *How wonderful it would be to watch his body relax, to see his tortured face become peaceful. To know he was pain-free, his agony over.*

My gaze moved to a large photo hanging on the wall above Dad's bed, a headshot of him and Mum taken in Glendalough. She was smiling, looking decades younger than him, despite the fact she was two years older. He was standing beside her, slightly stooped, a fancy red cravat hiding his tracheostomy. Hard to believe it had been taken only a few months before.

I looked at Dad. He'd fallen asleep again, the track of a dried tear visible down one cheek, his laboured, rasping breaths extra loud in the quiet of the night. Returning the excess tablets to the bottle, I gently woke him and placed the prescribed two small tablets on his tongue. Holding the straw to his lips, I watched him swallow, my chest tightening, crushing me as he took the final gulp. *I'd missed my chance.* Sleep evaded me as I agonised at my cowardice. *Did I love him too much, or not enough?*

The brightness of morning brought no relief from my guilt and regret. Dad didn't stir as I placed a kiss on his forehead before leaving for work. His face was flushed. Was it my imagination, or did his breathing sound more tortured than ever? As I drove, my view was blurred by tears, my heart aching with a sadness no 21-year-old should know. My cries of guilt and despair at my missed opportunity the night before filled the car. *When would this hell be over?* And as I asked myself that question, I began to cry all over again as I wondered how I would live in a world without Dad.

Just two days later, on 9 October 1987, at 9 a.m. while I was at work, it ended. There was no fanfare as Dad slipped away, no family gathered to wave him off. But perhaps the ending was all that it should have been, as he took his final breath with just one witness by his side: his closest companion and dearest friend, Mum. However, it remains one of my greatest regrets not to have been there to say goodbye, to give one final kiss, to whisper 'I love you' one last time.

11

I Confess

In the months after Dad died, Mum got great comfort from religion, whereas I did not. Growing up, religion had always been important to her. We were raised Catholic, went to mass every week, gave up chocolate and sweets for Lent and were taught that we should avoid sin. Michael did his best to abide by all the rules, while I on the other hand was of a less compliant nature and not so fearful of the consequences. As long as Mum didn't catch me, I didn't much care what God might do, and if my sins did stack up, I could always seek forgiveness in Confession.

Confession was something we went to at least two or three times a year, especially before Easter and Christmas. Due to my flippant nature, sins did not weigh particularly heavy on my mind, so it was only when I found myself sitting outside the confessional awaiting my turn to seek forgiveness that I would give any thought to my transgressions and begin to cherry pick the least of my sins to confess. *I told lies, I took the name of God in vain, and I was mean to my brother* – these were my standard lot for years. As I'd confess to the listening priest I'd have every intention of being a better person, but such intentions, especially about being nicer to Michael, rarely lasted more than a few hours.

I remember one such Confession when I was nine and Michael eight. Easter was approaching and the family was on holiday, staying at our grandparents' home in the village of Carrigart,

County Donegal. Coming from an estate of houses in Dublin, we relished our freedom on such holidays, every lane leading to adventure, every field our playground. Daily, Mike and I set off, with no instructions other than to stay away from the 'Black Hole' (local folklore deemed it to be a bottomless pool of water) and to be home for lunch or dinner. However, on this particular day our adventuring would have to wait as we'd been packed into the car for a family drive to one of Mum's favourite spots, Ards Forest Park.

My memories of visiting there each year are mixed. It was an idyllic setting, a 200-acre woodland with sandy beaches and rocky inlets for us to explore, a place where even as a child I could appreciate its beauty. However, it did have one major downside: within its grounds was the Franciscan Capuchin Friary, or a church, as I thought of it as a child. This meant that on every visit, our explorations and play were disrupted so that we could go in to say a prayer. Even worse, this afternoon Mum had discovered Confession was in progress, and it being Easter week, we all had to go.

Entering the small church, we could have sat almost anywhere, as it was close to empty, but we walked towards the altar and followed Mum into a pew. Kneeling beside Michael I put my head in my hands, pretending to pray as we waited our turn to go to Confession. Something about the hush and imposed silence in a church always ignited the giddy in me, but on this occasion Michael was an unwilling participant in my skittishness, ignoring my prods and pokes, his hands joined in prayer, looking every bit the devout worshipper. Bored and unable to concentrate on my prayers, I lifted my head and peeped over the pew at the door through which I would be going to confess my sins. I wondered why the usual Confession boxes around the church were missing and supposed they must be within that room. My stomach churned with a mixture of excitement and fear as my turn approached, until finally, Mum disappeared through the door. I was now at the end of the seat, next in line to go in – and in no doubt that I was in dire need of the loo! Judging by Michael's wiggling, he needed to go too.

Waiting for Mum to emerge, I wondered if there was a toilet anywhere. Between wiggles Michael peeked at me, his face flushed, possibly as he too was close to bursting, but I flashed him my older sister, *I haven't a care in the world* expression, closed my eyes and returned to my 'praying'. Mum seemed to be an age, and with every minute that passed my need for the toilet became critical. To distract myself, I began to rehearse the introduction to Confession I'd been taught at school, followed by my usual three sins: 'Bless me, father, for I have sinned, it is three months since my last Confession.' *Was it three months?* The door opened and Mum signalled for me to go in. I walked over, my full bladder forgotten as I wondered, *Do I knock, or just walk in?* I knocked. A muffled voice spoke from behind the door. I'd no idea what the voice said but I took it to be an invitation to enter. Cautiously, I turned the handle.

I cannot describe my alarm as I stepped into the room. It was small and blindingly bright compared to the darkness of the church. Alarmingly, there was no sign of a Confession box but instead were two chairs facing each other. Sitting in one of them was a rotund man, dressed in a brown cloak and wearing toeless sandals.

'Sit,' said the man, continuing to stare at his own toes.

Was he even a priest? I walked over and sat on the other chair, facing sideways so I didn't have to look at him. He said nothing, so I began to speak, my voice quivering. 'Bless me, father ...'

'Just get on with it,' he said.

I hesitated. *What did he mean? Did he want me to ditch my introduction?*

'Your sins,' he boomed, as if I'd been keeping him all day. 'Just tell me your sins.'

Well, if Jesus Christ himself had appeared and shouted at me I couldn't have been more shocked.

'ItookthenameofGodinvain,IItoldliesandIwas meantomybrother,' I rushed without a breath. Fortheseandallmyothersins ...' I hurried on.

But he interrupted me again. 'Say three Hail Marys, two Our Fathers and the Creed,' he said, before blessing me with the sign of the cross and mumbling some more.

I sat, waiting for him to stop speaking. *The Creed! All those prayers and the Creed!* I'd never heard of so much penance. His muttering stopped. I stood up, blessed myself and almost broke into a run as I made my way to the door. As soon as Michael saw me exit he jumped up, scanning my face for any clue as to how I'd got on. I bowed my head, joined my hands in prayer and passed him, the picture of holiness. However, once back in my seat I couldn't keep my giggles down as I pictured the scene on the other side of the door. I could only imagine Michael's horror at this unfamiliar set-up. Kneeling to begin my penance, I put my head in my hands, peeping regularly over the pew, eagerly anticipating his exit. The look on his eight-year-old bewildered, beetroot face as he emerged did not disappoint. I thought I might burst as I supressed my laughter.

He knelt beside me with his head down for a minute before we both looked at one another.

'I didn't like that priest,' he hissed, in the loud whisper of a child.

'Why?' I said, almost exploding.

'He wouldn't let me speak. I got all confused and had to keep starting again but he got cross.'

'Really?' I giggled. 'What penance did you get?'

'He gave me a million prayers *and* the Creed,' he said.

'Wow, you must have been very bold. I only got one Hail Mary,' I lied.

That memory never ceases to make me smile. The God of my childhood had been a kindly one, happy to regularly forgive me and willing to listen when I prayed for the teacher to not notice I'd no homework done or to escape detection when I'd broken something at home. He'd been a God who, Mum assured us, looked after little children and loved them. However, during my teens He and I parted ways and I stopped praying. Could God not hear as I prayed, *Please God, not today?* Did He not care when I begged Him to, *Make him stop*? At sixteen, I gave up on Him completely.

My final conversation with God came after a religious retreat organised by my school. All morning we were told about the love of God, the forgiveness of God and how wonderful it is to have God in your life. I listened, particularly touched by the middle-aged priest who had spoken about the kind, forgiving God. During the session we were given time to sit in silence with our thoughts but mine were torturing me, the memory of assaults and the hiding and lying deeply upsetting. Guilty and ashamed, my conscience was loud and vocal: *I am a liar, a bad person, a sinner.*

After an hour of soul-searching, I decided to pluck up the courage to speak with the priest who had spoken of forgiveness and had seemed so kind during the morning session. Heart pounding but resolute, I walked into Confession and sat opposite him, beginning just as I had as a young child in Ards: 'Bless me, father, for I have sinned.'

My voice shaking, my face on fire, I told my secret for the first time, the words pouring out. 'Sex'. 'Married man'. 'I want it to end.' I had barely begun when I stopped, sensing the hostility in the room. There was no trace of the friendly priest who'd addressed the class earlier that morning. His reaction was merciless. I was a sinner, he raged. What I'd confessed to was a mortal sin. He was almost apoplectic as he ranted on, every word slicing through me. By the time he began to tell me what a bad person I was, I'd heard enough and walked out.

Returning to my friends, I put my everyday face on, but inside I was shaking, his words continuing to wound me. He'd confirmed what I had most feared: *it was my fault. I was a bad person.* We had numerous other group lessons that afternoon, but thankfully none with the priest I'd 'confessed' to. While the others debated and discussed various topics, I was quiet, not participating as I had that morning, his words tormenting me. *Was I a bad person? Was it my fault?*

That evening, as the retreat came to an end, the priest I had trusted with my secret gathered us for final prayers. Real or imagined, I was convinced he was looking at me. Like a rebellious teenager I lounged in my chair, legs outstretched, arms folded, eyeballing him back as he spoke.

'You must never forget that Jesus will always be there for you in your future lives,' he said, he and I staring at one another. 'But know that there are some people, even within our midst, so full of sin there is no helping them.'

Up to that moment I had felt like a sinner, his words from earlier having cut deep. However, listening to him pontificate as I sat among my friends, something inside me snapped. My shame gave way to a tremendous fury – at that priest, at his church and at Gibney.

That evening, God and I parted ways and we have never spoken since. Yet, I have no lingering anger towards a God I no longer believe in or towards that priest, or priests in general. I am not anti-religion. It is just not for me. Looking back, I know that it was not just that priest but many other priests and lay people in 1980s Ireland who were ill-informed. Telling anyone back then, be they strangers, family or friends, was always a gamble, and unfortunately there were quite a number whose reaction was not what I would have wished.

Thankfully, Eamonn was not among them. From the moment I told him what had happened to me, by then a wife and young mother, he has been steadfast in his support, always taking his lead from me, never pushing for information or asking too much, but quietly prevailing, without judgement or display of hurt or anger. My rock.

12

Becoming a Mother

I grew up in a time of fairy tales where no one questioned princes and princesses, and happy ever after was how everything ended. Perhaps I was ahead of my time, but I didn't dream of a prince, and while I enjoyed reading those stories, the child in me never saw a princess in herself. I loved all things 'boy' and could climb any tree faster – and go higher – than most of the boys on our road. I had no qualms about physically fighting anyone who challenged me. Gender equality was a lesser-known concept back then: some days if the boys were short of numbers they let me play football, but more often I was told, 'No girls allowed.' Furious at such unfairness, I'd wait until the ball came out of play and race off with it, making sure to give it a good kick down the road moments before I was caught.

But as well as this aggressive, competitive side, there was also a softer me. A girl who, from the earliest age, loved to mother, my dolls as real to me as if they were family as I washed, dressed and cared for them. They were my fellow actors in fantasy tales which may have lacked princes and princesses, but were full of happy ever after.

The passing of time did nothing to quench my maternal instinct, and my desire for children reached a peak just weeks after Eamonn and I married in 1990. It was not a desire shared by Eamonn at the time, pointing out our relative youth: I was twenty-four, and he twenty-nine.

Unfortunately for him, it was too early in our marriage for him to know he wasn't equipped to argue with me. As I relentlessly pressed home my point, I blinded him with science, insisting it could take us years. Within weeks I was pregnant.

It's fair to say we were both shocked and surprised, but we couldn't wait for the arrival of our bundle, its due date our first wedding anniversary. From the moment I'd set eyes on that blue line on the pregnancy test I'd bonded with this child.

'It's a boy,' I told Eamonn, as sure as if I'd had a scan. 'Women just know these things. It's intuition.'

He wasn't convinced, and cautioned me for buying so many blue items of clothing. I tolerated his scepticism, assuring him I knew what I was doing. Finally, four days overdue and after a difficult labour I delivered our baby: a perfect little girl! We called her Aoife.

The months that followed were the best of times and the worst of times. The shock of a new baby was something neither of us was prepared for, and the tiredness something we will never forget. My thirst for motherhood was well and truly quenched, but regardless of the many challenges, my heart was full, with so much love for my baby.

However, beneath the surface something had changed. Looking in the mirror I tried to identify what it was. Although a little weary, I looked like me. My body was returning to its pre-pregnancy shape but inside I felt different – less, not more. Weakened, damaged, fragile, frightened. Lying awake at night, Eamonn and Aoife sleeping soundly beside me, I felt alone and troubled. Fearful, but I didn't know of what. This wasn't the way it was meant to be. By day I waited, wondering if someone would notice, but no one did.

When Aoife was eight months old my brother Ben and his then wife Maria came to visit. They had returned from living in Papua New Guinea, where their first baby, Claire, had been born, three weeks before our little girl. As I sat listening to my sister-in-law describe her baby's birth, I was struck by how different our experiences were.

'I felt empowered,' she said, obviously still feeling it.

Really? I thought.

Later that night, as I lay awake in the dark, I thought back on what Maria had said, and it hit me just how traumatised I'd been since the birth. In that moment, alone in the darkness, I finally found the words to describe what I'd been feeling: *It felt as if I'd been raped.*

Little did I know that, in that moment of clarity, a wound I couldn't see, which had been bleeding silently since I'd given birth, burst open. The bolt on a secret door, somewhere in the far recess of my mind, had been pulled back and the door opened, never to close again. Behind this door lurked the villain of my teenage years, George Gibney, the man I'd put out of my mind for seven years, the secret I had never told anyone. Now that I'd opened the door, I'd no control over when Gibney would appear, his face, his beard, his smell only a thought away. Driving my car, nursing my baby or waking in the night, I'd see him, always for just the briefest of moments. A close-up of his face or a fleeting feeling of terror, imagining I felt his touch rough on my skin or that I heard him speak. He was back, inhabiting my mind and body, and I was finding it impossible to keep him away.

And as he took control, I lost it. Quietly, in full view of a loving husband and many friends, I sank into a world they knew nothing about, returning to the isolation of my teenage years, alone with my secrets of childhood. *Why didn't I tell anyone? I was an adult, with a husband who loved me. Why not tell?* Because when you keep a secret so long the words hide with it. There is no right time to tell, only wrong times. My secret was huge for me, but well hidden behind stone walls of my own making, enormous walls that had taken years to build. No one could share my secret unless I let them in, and if I did that it would mean letting him out. Who would choose to liberate a monster?

As I struggled through those days and nights, I had no idea that a bomb was on its way which would blow those walls to pieces. That bomb was being assembled in Dublin by my childhood friend Gary O'Toole, whom I'd lost all those years before.

13

The Bombshell

Dear Patricia, I'm writing to you about things that might have happened to you whilst we were swimming together in Trojan and things that George Gibney might have done to you. If you know nothing about what I might be talking to you about, do NOT open the letter on the inside of this envelope, but if you know what I'm talking about, please open this letter.

By the time we were celebrating Aoife's first birthday, the flashbacks and memories I was experiencing were more frequent and becoming increasingly difficult to ignore. Picking her up in her cot, changing her nappy or giving her a bath, I'd imagine I'd glimpsed Gibney's face in the mirror or sensed him by my side. It was only the briefest of moments, never long enough to process, but enough to leave me feeling unsettled. At night in my dreams I ran for my life, not knowing from what, or watched as an enormous wave crashed over my head, submerging me, before I woke gasping for breath. I excused my nightmares, telling myself they were the result of a broken sleep, the perils of being the mother of a one-year-old, but a part of me knew; my walls were becoming weak, my secret was seeping out. Furiously, by day I did my best to rebuild those walls, actively blotting out or dismissing the flashbacks and nightmares and never telling a soul, as I fought hard to keep my secret. However, little did I know that such efforts would be in vain, as weeks after Aoife's first birthday the bombshell arrived in the form of a letter, carefully worded and written by Gary. A letter which would spark a whole new set of nightmares.

In December 1990, Gary was on a plane to Australia with the Irish team, when Chalkie White, a coach on the trip, had the courage to speak out and tell him that he had been abused by Gibney as a young boy. It was a lot for a 22-year-old to take in, and over the next few months, as Gary processed what he had heard, he wondered about the teenage girls he had swum with whose friendships he had lost. Friendships such as mine. Over the next year Gary left Trojan and began to further investigate Chalkie's allegation, wondering how best to proceed as his concerns fell on deaf ears.

Not willing to look away, but not wanting to intrude, in 1992 Gary wrote me that letter and sent it by registered post. I'd never received a registered letter before. For a moment I sat at the kitchen table scanning the envelope for clues as to what it might be, or who it might be from, never for a minute suspecting the life-changing effect its contents would have.

Opening the envelope, I discovered two letters inside, one of which was in a second, sealed, envelope. As I read the cover letter Gary had written, my heart ran cold, the words *George Gibney* jumping out at me from the page. As real as if I'd opened my door to him, he morphed in front of me, just a few feet from where I was standing, his dark eyes leering at me from behind his glasses, his teeth visible from within his beard as he grinned. His smirk stabbing a hot rod into my chest, puncturing my lungs. I struggled to breathe, the air around me filled with his sickly-sweet aftershave, as strong and odorous as if he were once more on top of me. I shook my head to blink him away, before reading Gary's letter once more.

'If you know what I'm talking about, please open this letter.'

Shaking, I reached for the second envelope,

pausing for just a moment before tearing it open, reading it hurriedly. The words *George Gibney ... abuse ... statements ... guards ... counsellor* sending a chill through my entire body.

I sank into one of the chairs at the kitchen table, put my face in my hands and closed my eyes, but I couldn't un-see the letter, its words dancing before me, his name in bold. Deep within my soul a small voice began to scream, and in the silence of my kitchen those screams, from the child I'd once been, blended with the rasping sobs of the young mother I'd become. Hysteria overwhelmed me and I began to shiver uncontrollably. My stomach heaved and I rushed to the sink, staring into the basin. *Breathe,* I told myself. *One long breath in ... one longer breath out.* A few breaths later my nausea lessened, and the screaming stopped.

I turned around and looked at the letters sitting on the table behind me, their words echoing in my head: *guards ... statements ... George Gibney.* Unwilling to be near them, I walked into the sitting room, but the letters followed. My past had found me, ready or not.

Heart pounding, I returned to the kitchen. From the door, I stood looking at the letters lying open on the table, their envelope with my address clearly visible beside them. Walking into the kitchen I picked them up, my anger rising as I crunched them into a ball before throwing them in the bin under the sink, slamming the cupboard door shut. I walked away but could still feel their presence. Taking them out again I went outside and threw them in the large household rubbish bin at the back of the house, but as I returned to the kitchen they followed me, their words seeping out, surrounding me in memories as years of secrets, lies, fear and loneliness consumed me. The words were out, Gary shouting them, Eamonn questioning them, Gibney laughing at them. I did not want them in my house.

Retrieving them from the bin, I rushed to my car, my hands shaking as I opened its passenger door and shoved both letters into the glove compartment, burying them under a mishmash of bibs and sweet wrappers. Adrenaline flowing, I rushed upstairs, pausing to catch my breath outside one-year-old Aoife's bedroom, the mother I'd become kicking in, urging the panicked child within me to calm down.

Quietly, I opened the bedroom door and stood for a moment over my baby's cot, watching her sleep, her gentle snores the necessary salve to my panic. Reaching in, I picked her up, breathing in the sweet smell of her sleep. She barely stirred as she placed her head on my shoulder and nuzzled into my neck. Warm tears spilled down my face as a wave of protective fury replaced my fear. This baby was my life. That bastard Gibney had no place in my home.

I carried my half-asleep baby downstairs and strapped her into her car seat before driving the few minutes to my friend Olive's house, the letters ticking loudly within their hiding place. Arriving, I reached over and pulled them out, spilling the contents of the glove compartment to the floor in my haste. Leaving Aoife, who had resumed her sleep, in her car seat, I stumbled into Olive's and thrust the letters into her hands.

'What is it?' she asked, startled by my arrival and distress.

'A letter. I don't want it in my house.'

'Who's it from?'

'It doesn't matter, I just don't want it. Will you keep it here?' I pleaded, my tears saying more than I could. Hugging me, she assured me she would. She was the first of very few who would hear of my secret but never pry.

Anxious to return home and leave the letters behind, I left quickly, telling her I'd call her later. Now that they were gone, I hoped I could forget about them, but as I opened my front door, I knew it was not going to be that easy. Immediately I sensed a change in the house. My home no longer felt like the sanctuary it once was. Gibney was there, in every room, in every thought. I put the radio and television on, trying to drown him out, with little success. Later, when Eamonn returned home from work, I put in an Oscar-winning performance as I chit-chatted about my 'ordinary' day. However, as one day went to two and I still had not told him, it became more and more difficult to pretend. Where once the monster had lived in darkness, so rarely glimpsed I'd wondered if I'd imagined his appearance, now he roamed free, reminding me by day that he had not gone away and in the darkness of night hurting me all over again.

In the aftermath of the letter, I quickly realised what a good job I'd done of supressing my abuse by Gibney. The flashbacks and memories triggered by Aoife's birth were upsetting but not overwhelming, and I'd never felt the need to tell Eamonn or anyone my secret. Now, however, the letter was all I could think about and I began to regret my haste in handing it over to my friend Olive. *Had I read it correctly? Did it say there were others? That I was not the only one?* I knew I had to read it again, so I retrieved it.

Since first reading it, fragments of memories,

long forgotten, had begun to surface, but I was not willing to entertain them. These were different to the flashbacks, being my own conscious thoughts and rememberings rather than something sprung on me. Opening the envelope, I read the letter again. *Yes, there were other victims. I was not the only one!* I sat for some time trying to get my head around it. There were others! I knew I should have felt something – rage, sadness, hurt – but I felt nothing.

For some time, I sat reading and re-reading it before hiding it away in my bedside locker. Several times over the next couple of days I thought about showing it to Eamonn, but I couldn't bring myself to do it. *What would I say to him? What would he think?* That he might feel compassion for me never entered my mind. As the days passed, more and more memories of what Gibney had done to me emerged, swamping me as I watched television, fed Aoife or lay awake in the night. My initial numbness wore off and I grew increasingly angry, until finally, after a senseless burst of rage one evening, Eamonn asked me what was wrong. I broke down and went to fetch the letter.

'Here. Read that,' I said, thrusting it into his hands without ceremony.

Prior to that moment, Eamonn would have presumed he knew me well, that he and I were soulmates. After five years and a baby together, he had no idea that the memories of my childhood and the past that I'd shared with him had been so highly edited. As he began to read the letter, I left the room, and when I returned, my silence made it clear that I was not willing to answer any questions.

For days, it remained the elephant in the room between us as I ignored the letter's existence, expecting Eamonn to know and immediately understand all that had happened with Gibney and how I was feeling. As is his way, Eamonn asked no questions and demanded no answers. Instead he stayed quietly watching from the sideline as I moved away, withdrawing to the island of my teenage years, unwilling to speak of the letter or what it contained.

This island of mine wasn't a sad place but rather somewhere safe, where I could hide and lick wounds no one could see. A sanctuary away from everyone, where I could be the person I knew I was, not what I thought others might believe me to be. Fragile, and afraid of what Eamonn might be thinking, I set about rebuilding my island walls and attacking him if he came too close, just wishing to be left alone.

However, this time my island was different to when I was a teenager. I was no longer alone, as no matter how far away I tried to go, my daughter followed, her baby giggles and adoring hugs chipping away at my walls before I had a chance to cement them in place. As they slowly crumbled, Eamonn patiently waited, his quiet strength and undemanding love ever ready to guide me over the rubble and back home, whenever I was ready.

Returning wasn't easy. The letter and its contents were all I could think of. With my

emerging memories came feelings of deep shame
and guilt. My secret was out. Gary knew. Eamonn
knew. Yet despite my world being flipped upside
down, I couldn't ignore the letter. It spoke about
more than what had happened to me. It told me
it had happened to others, that Gibney was even
more of a monster than I'd imagined. While my
initial thoughts on its arrival had been consumed
by horror and shame, as the weeks passed I began
to feel a fury I could not articulate, a hatred so
deep it ate away inside me. *How had Gibney found
the time to ruin other lives when he was stalking and
abusing me? How many years had he been doing this?
And worst of all, was he still doing it? Was someone
else now a victim because I had moved on?*

'I'm going to the guards,' I blurted out to
Eamonn after dinner one evening, surprising
even myself with my announcement. I had no
idea of the personal cost that decision would have
on my life and that of my families, nor could I
have dreamt that, by coming forward with other
survivors, we were about to open a Pandora's box

on Irish swimming that would spotlight many more stolen childhoods and uncover a further two paedophiles in the sport. Unlike the survivors of George Gibney, those survivors would get their day in court. Olympic swim coach Derry O'Rourke was sentenced to twelve years in jail for twenty-nine charges relating to eleven girls under the age of fifteen. He received a further ten-year sentence in a subsequent trial five years later for the rape and sexual assault of another girl.

Ger Doyle was sentenced to six-and-a-half years in prison for thirty-five sex-related charges against five boys aged ten to fifteen.

As I announced my decision, I immediately felt lighter. *Bring it on,* I thought, as Eamonn hugged me. I sensed his pride in my decision and was fortified. *I will get that bastard.*

14

Haunted

I summoned the courage to phone one of the two numbers in Gary's letter and made an appointment with a psychologist in Dublin. I wasn't sure what good talking to him would do but it was an easier first step than ringing the second number Gary had sent, which was the superintendent in Blackrock garda station. The psychologist agreed to see me within days, so, leaving Aoife with Olive, while Eamonn was at work, I took the train to Dublin.

Mum was surprised to hear I was coming to

stay for a night without Eamonn and Aoife. So too was Eamonn, but I wanted to do this by myself. Sitting in the kitchen of 108 opposite Mum, it was as if I were a teenager once more, my secret filling the space between us, but I knew I couldn't tell her. *What would I say? Why would I upset her?*

Mum was no fool and sensed this was not a regular visit, regardless of how I parcelled it up. A couple of times she made general inquiries as to whether everything in Cork was okay and if I was well, but I assured her all was good and that I was just in need of a break.

She went along with my lies but as I kissed her goodnight, she said in her most gentle, motherly voice, 'What's wrong, Trish?'

For the briefest of moments I was tempted, so very tempted, to tell her, wanting nothing more than to be held in her arms and comforted, but as quickly as I'd thought about it I changed my mind, reverting to my usual manner of deflection: attack.

'Oh, for God's sake, Mum, can I not come to

Dublin to visit you without you thinking there's something wrong?'

It worked, as it had many times before. She said no more, and I stomped upstairs to the bedroom of my childhood and a sleepless night surrounded by memories of the past.

My appointment was the following afternoon. If Mum was suspicious the day before, I can only imagine what she thought about the level of distraction I exhibited as the morning ticked by. I tried to prepare myself for what might lie ahead, picturing myself sitting in the waiting room and greeting the psychologist. However, to imagine what our conversation might be was a step too far, so I didn't even try. As the time to leave 108 came, I was almost sick with dread.

At the front door, Mum hugged me extra tightly. 'Good luck, Trish, with whatever it is you are going to.' I saw her eyes fill with tears.

Taken aback, I muttered, 'Thanks', and walked away quickly, so she wouldn't see mine do the same.

My meeting with the psychologist remains hidden somewhere in the depths of my memory. I can't picture his office or what he looked like, but I know I told him I'd got in touch with him because of a letter from Gary and that Gibney had abused me. I recall him sitting near me, saying he had met one of the other victims, and I remember him speaking of guilt and fear. However, as he did so I felt nothing, his words falling into the space between us. It was as if I was watching from outside my body, listening to him speak with someone else. Then it was over, and I was on the train home to Cork.

Initially I was relieved to be on my way, but as the hours passed and the carriage emptied, I began to process some of what the psychologist had said, hearing it afresh. It was as if he had torn the scab off a wound, picking into it, leaving an open sore, paining me. I tried not to think of it, but it was gross and not something I wanted on view. I was angry, but at what exactly I wasn't sure, and couldn't sit still, my fists clenching and unclenching. I was itching to thump something or someone as guilt, disgust and anger ran riot inside me. Pressing my head against the cool window, I looked out into the darkness, tears spilling down my face. I wiped them away, confused as to where they came from as I did not feel sad. Reflected in the window I saw a middle-aged gentleman in the seat opposite, looking at me.

'WHAT?' I roared, spinning around to look at him. 'WHAT THE FUCK ARE YOU LOOKING AT?' I almost spat, in a surge of fury I had not foreseen.

He didn't reply but quickly picked up his bag and walked out of the carriage. I knew there were a couple of other passengers sitting further up but I didn't care; shouting had felt good, but the relief was only temporary. Arriving into Cork, it didn't take Eamonn long to judge my mood and he wisely left me to my thoughts.

Over the next few days holes began to appear in the vault of my locked-away memories, allowing voices, images, smells and feelings to seep out. Like shovelling snow in a snowstorm, I tried to push them back, but Gibney lurked in my every day, appearing unannounced in vivid confusing and frightening flashbacks, taking over my thinking, demanding I remember. Despite all the love and support I got from Eamonn and the couple of friends who knew, I rarely confided in them the horrors of my days or nights, although occasionally it would become too much for me to bear and I would tell them about the flashbacks.

On hearing this, they would nod sympathetically or give me a hug. But how could they know? How could anyone know what is meant by a flashback without ever having experienced one?

In those early days my flashbacks were just as the name suggests: a flash, a nanosecond where Gibney's bespectacled, goatee-bearded face appeared, or I heard his low, quiet voice. Startled, I'd blink away the vision, or distract myself and carry on, shaken but not too bothered. However, the flashes soon became more than that and as they did, my fear of them began to take over my days and nights. One of the first times I remember experiencing a longer flashback was one afternoon, at home with Aoife, days after Gary's letter arrived.

I am twenty-six years old, and Aoife is a toddling one-year-old bundle of fun, rarely more than a step behind me, babbling continuously. I am her world, and she is mine. I have just picked her up from her nap, and I put her down in the playroom and watch her run in delight towards the basket full of teddies. Leaving her in the toy-strewn room, I open the door to my kitchen and as I do, I enter George Gibney's office. Before me are its walls, his desk, the carpet and large window shaded by blinds, as real as they once were. Pure fear jolts through me: there he is, grinning at me from behind his desk. The drum of my racing heart beats loudly in my ears as he stands up and walks around the desk towards me, obviously pleased by my arrival. I freeze, my body ignoring my silent screams to run as I desperately try to blink him away. He's not here, I tell myself as a cold chill envelops me. He comes closer and I can't look away. I see his face, his glasses, his beard, his smirk. He's within touching distance. Smelling distance. Breathe ... In ... Out ...

And then he is gone. Vanished in an instant. Yet I feel no relief. The child in me trembles, as the adult in me tries to console her. It was your imagination, I reassure myself, looking around the freshly transformed kitchen, as if he might still be there. Oh my God! He'd seemed so real. Am I going mad?

The sound of Aoife's baby chattering brings me back to the moment. Reaching to pick her up I hold her close, as a wave of anger comes and I chastise myself for being so afraid of a memory. That bastard can fuck off. Turning the CD player up high I dance

around the floor, my little lady giggling in
delight in my arms, the perfect antidote to
my fear and anger.

Going to bed after a day peppered by such flashbacks
terrified me. As darkness fell and the house became
quiet, I had no such luxury as a blaring CD player
or chattering toddler to distract me. I dreaded
closing my eyes, fearing his arrival as I slept.

'You coming to bed?' Eamonn would say, and
I'd die a little inside as the charade of our night-
time routine began.

'No, I think I'll stay here a little longer,' I'd
reply, stretching out on the couch, flicking
between the five free channels on our portable
19-inch television.

'Will I turn out any lights?'

'No, I'll do it,' I'd tell him, knowing I wouldn't,
fearing the darkness.

On those nights, as I listened to the creaking
boards of Eamonn getting ready for bed, there
was an agony in my solitude, a bleak hopelessness

for the future. I felt damaged, and wondered was I allowing myself go a little crazy. I'd sit upright instead of slouching on the couch, and I'd turn off the heat, hoping the cold would keep me awake, the television permanently on for company. Tired and exhausted from lack of sleep and mothering a one-year-old, it was impossible to keep my eyes open. Waking, moments or hours later, I'd jump up, horrified that I'd slept yet grateful that he hadn't appeared in my dreams. During those nights it felt as if I were the only person in the world awake. Sometimes I'd cry quietly without knowing why, only that I was sad, while on other nights I was consumed with rage, wanting to smash all around me. Occasionally my fury would be so overwhelming I'd have to leave the house to walk it off, almost welcoming the idea of being attacked in the dim light of midnight on our estate, more than ready to fight back, relishing the thought of battering someone.

However, on other nights the guilt I felt at Eamonn sleeping alone got to me. I knew he didn't expect me to come upstairs, but I also knew that any night I did, it helped him think I was doing okay, and I desperately wanted him to believe that. So, especially after a day with no major flashbacks, I'd feel a little braver and tiptoe on up, listening at my little one's door before going into bed.

Entering our bedroom, I was always grateful to Eamonn for having left the light on, just in case I'd appear. Regardless of how late the hour, he'd register my arrival with a kiss or a gentle squeeze of my hand, quietly acknowledging my achievement and reassuring me that he was there for me. Lying beside him, I'd envy his speedy return to sleep, appreciating the luxury of lying in bed on a soft pillow covered with a duvet, as opposed to sitting in the cold on the couch downstairs. *Maybe tonight I'd have no nightmares?* But, inevitably, in the solitude of sleep, he came.

It's late at night and I'm standing in a dimly lit car park, my every nerve on high alert as I sense Gibney near. Where is he? I creep forward, ducking behind cars as I look for a way out, tip-toeing as I go, terrified he might hear me breathing.

'Hi there.'

Out of the shadows, he steps in front of me, so close I breathe in the warm, foul breath he breathes out. He stands there, his face inches from mine. I freeze, too frightened to move. Tonight he speaks, his voice low and quiet as he threatens, ridicules and laughs at me. Suddenly I feel his hands squeezing my arms, his foot kicking mine out of the way, dragging me to the ground. Helpless to move, I lie pinned beneath him, his beard scraping my face, the weight of him making it difficult to breathe.

Panting, I wake, searching for my escape, the lights of the bedroom confusing, until I realise it is a nightmare. Have I been screaming? *Eamonn is sleeping peacefully beside me. He has asked me to wake him after such events, but I never do. It takes time to return to calm, to convince myself it never happened. I have no desire to go back to sleep. Even in the brief darkness of a blink Gibney's face grins back at me. I must stay awake. Yet despite my determination I doze off, sometimes only to immediately slip into another nightmare.*

Waking the next morning, the horror of my nightmares was as palpable as if they had been real. In the bathroom I scanned the face looking back at me in the mirror, checking for signs of the scratches that I felt stinging my cheek, before wandering downstairs to face the day.

'Did you sleep okay?' Eamonn asked.

'Ye, thanks,' I lied.

As the days passed, I despaired, wondering would I ever again enjoy a day or night without the worry of flashbacks or nightmares. *Was it the fear of going to the guards that triggered them? Maybe when that was over they would end?*

15

Precious
Memories

Three weeks had passed since Mark and I had first sat in my kitchen to discuss the podcast and I was once again nervously pacing the floor watching the clock as I waited for him to arrive. He'd emailed a few days before to ask if I was still okay to be recorded, and I'd replied that I was. But I wasn't. Why would I put myself through it? Or put Mum and my family through it? Yet here I was, minutes away from welcoming him and his cursed mic into my home.

Bang on time he arrived, and I welcomed him as if I were delighted to see him. However, as he placed a large microphone on the table and clipped a tiny one to my top, I confessed to him that I was unhappy and had been having serious second thoughts.

'I'm still going to go ahead,' I said, 'but if you had left it just one more week, I would have pulled out.'

Grateful I had not, I sat with Mark for a while as he once again spoke to me of the reasons behind the podcast and assured me it was not to make victims out of us. One cup of tea later I was ready, but as the recording began, I felt myself stiffen. Whereas before, Mark and I had chatted freely, now I was more measured, guarded, wary. It was one thing to share my story with him but another to speak it knowing it would be heard by an audience of strangers. However, over time I began to relax and open up about some of those traumatic memories. It was a long afternoon.

Later that night as I lay in bed my mind was spinning as I tried to recall some of what I had told Mark. Would it be too much for the kids to hear? What about Eamonn and my family? Vivid memories of what I'd shared filled my head. Surely they would trigger nightmares. I began to read, fearful that the sights and sounds of the past would overwhelm me and that Gibney would visit in the night, but thankfully I slept soundly.

A few days later my cousin Eileen texted me and all thoughts of the podcast and Mark were forgotten. Mum was unwell again with another infection. I was inconsolable. She had only begun to recover, to regain her strength. I couldn't see how her body would cope with this latest setback so soon after the last life-threatening one. Distraught, I packed for Dublin, not knowing how long I'd be staying.

'Hopefully I'll be back by the weekend, for my birthday,' I said to Eamonn and my children as

I waved goodbye, but I wasn't convinced. At the back of my mind I couldn't shake the thought, *This is it.*

Driving to Dublin, all the different scenarios went through my head. *Maybe it won't be as bad this time? What if she's in hospital by the end of the day? What if she refuses to go to hospital?*

It seemed so unfair the way life was turning out for Mum. For two years she'd fought uphill battles against broken bones and infections. How long could she keep fighting? Safe in the solitude of my car, I cried, sobbing aloud as I imagined one day in the future going home to 108 without her warm welcome to greet me, of never again laughing with her or enjoying an afternoon of chat. I knew I was being selfish, but I wanted more time, even if it were only a few more weeks.

I remembered the final weeks with Dad. The future we had imagined with him had been wiped out with his diagnosis. However, we discovered that instead of the days flying by, as the end of his life approached, the opposite occurred.

With no guarantees of a tomorrow, every minute of every day became more and more precious. I'd got to spend treasured moments with him, sitting beside his bed sharing my everyday life in a way a twenty-one-year-old never would do with a parent. By being told our time together was short, we were in fact being granted time. I needed to remember that now. Mum's clock might be winding down but it was still ticking, and it was up to me to make the most of what we had left.

Three days later we knew that Mum's time was indeed preciously short. The infection was serious, and having discussed it with her GP she'd made her intentions clear: she was not going to hospital. We understood and respected her request although it was a difficult one to accept, especially as the previous day and during the night she had been particularly restless and unwell. We'd taken the night in shifts and Michael was 'on duty' as I woke at 7 a.m. with a feeling of dread for what the day might bring.

It was 17 March 2019, St Patrick's Day, also

my birthday. Just two days earlier Mum had gone to bed feeling tired and unwell, hoping she'd be better the next day. She had not improved nor left her bed, yet she still had planned a lovely birthday breakfast for me, and the previous night had directed Eileen to leave out the clothes she wished to wear. Outside her bedroom door I hesitated, preparing myself for how she might look, perhaps semi-conscious or as ill as she had been when I left her a few hours before. Quietly, I pushed the door open.

The lights in her bedroom were on and she was sitting up in bed, bright-eyed and alert, Michael brushing her hair.

'Happy Birthday,' she said, with the biggest smile, throwing out her arms to me. I rushed towards them and she hugged me tight. It was the greatest present I've ever received.

'This was the day you and I first met,' she said, and I lay there holding her gently, more grateful for this gift of time than I've ever been for anything in my life.

However, it was not an easy day. The clothes

Mum had picked out with such hope and plans the day before stayed on the chair. She would not be wearing them today. Nor would she be getting up. We tried to pretend it wasn't a big deal, keeping the mood light as we ate my birthday breakfast in the room with her, but when she and I were finally alone her mask slipped.

'This is it, Trish,' she said, reaching for both of my hands as I sat on the bed beside her.

'Do you think so?' I replied, a steady stream of tears pouring down my face. 'Maybe you're just exhausted, Mum, after being so unwell yesterday? A few more days and you might feel better?'

'No, Trish. I know,' she said, and I could hear the resignation in her voice.

My chest was on fire, the pain so acute it caught my breath. I squeezed her hands and leaned forward, resting my cheek next to hers. It was the saddest of moments as we sat there quietly crying our silent goodbye. I was desperate to tell her to keep fighting but I knew it would be wrong to ask any more from her. Eventually I pulled back and reached for a tissue from the box on her bed, taking out one for each of us.

'Don't tell the others,' she said as she dried her eyes.

'Okay, but they might suspect something when they see the state of me,' I said, trying to work a miracle on my blotchy red face.

Over the next few days Mum's clock wound down slowly, and as it did, she herself spoke with Eileen and the family, saying her goodbyes, and also a teary one to Ruth, one of the much-loved children she'd minded many years before, and to Maureen and Valerie, her two best friends. It was a desperately painful process but as she discussed her upcoming death, she did so with a contentment that was beautiful to watch. She had a strong faith, but I hadn't realised just how strong until she told me that in the thirty-two years since Dad had died, she'd said hundreds of prayers at night as she went to sleep, and had no doubt there was an afterlife.

'I cannot wait to see John again,' she said many

times in those final days, and each time she said it her face lit up and there was an obvious glint of excitement in her eyes. It made our sad goodbye so much easier.

In the days after my birthday Mum slept a lot, but one morning, returning from the chemist, I found her sitting up looking more alert than she had in days. Michael was sitting beside her and as I entered the room she announced that it was time to plan the funeral mass. Mike and I looked at one another.

'Eh,' said Michael, 'I think you're asking the wrong two people.'

We laughed, reminding her that we knew next to nothing about mass, but she was insistent. She began with the funeral hymns. Mike opened his phone and, knowing Mum's taste in music better than I did, began to play different songs. It was excruciatingly painful, and I cried openly as Mum lay back, listening and commenting on each one.

'No, definitely not that one.' Or, 'Maybe?'

Then Michael said, 'I know this is the one,

Mum,' and he pressed play, putting the phone up to her ear.

As the sound of Slim Whitman singing 'Precious Memories' filled the room, Mum closed her eyes. 'I love that one,' she said.

'Oh please, Mum!' I said, inconsolable as I listened to the words. 'That song is way too sad. Look at the state of me listening to it. I'll never be able to get through the funeral.'

She opened her eyes and looked at me as the mother I'd always known, strong and determined. 'Patricia, don't let me down,' she said, more as a threat than a request.

I smiled through my tears as Michael piped in how he would definitely not let her down, re-enacting our old childhood rivalry.

'I'll try, Mum,' I said, 'but this is all so sad.'

'Patricia,' she said, smiling and reaching for my hand, 'just imagine, when that song is playing, John and I will be waltzing together.'

Five days later, on the twenty-ninth of March, I sat without shedding a tear, as Slim Whitman's

'Precious Memories' filled the church. As it played, in my mind's eye I watched the beautiful young woman she was and the man she adored waltz around the altar, finally reunited after thirty-two years.

Waking up the following day, my first thoughts were to wonder how Mum slept, before reality slapped me hard. She was gone. Over and over that day I repeated those words, barely able to take in the magnitude of what I was saying, as I saw her empty chair in the kitchen, her phone which no longer needed charging and Katie, her much-loved dog, looking for her in her bedroom. Although I told myself it was true, that Mum was indeed gone, it was impossible to grasp the reality of her not being around.

16

Doll's House

The day after Mum's funeral was her eighty-eighth birthday and the day after that, Mother's Day — a double whammy of sadness and loss. Eamonn and my children had been by my side every step of the past few days, on hand with a cup of tea or a kind word, a hug or a kiss, but now it was time for them to go, to get back to living. While my world had stopped, theirs continued to turn. I knew that mine would one day begin again, but I needed more time. Time to spend Mum's birthday with her and then Mother's Day, not as a mother but as a daughter. After that I'd say my goodbyes to 108 and try to pick up my own life again, but I couldn't imagine how.

After they left, the house was quiet, with just Eileen and me there. I put on the kettle, more to break the silence of the kitchen than the want of a cup of tea. No brothers and sisters and their families buzzing around, no visitors, no friends, no Mum. *This is the way it will be from now on.* Suddenly, desperate to feel Mum's presence, fearing she was already slipping from my memory, I went into her bedroom and closed the door. I took a deep breath, hoping to inhale her, to feel her seep into my soul and rekindle glorious memories, but all I could feel was her absence. I walked into her en-suite, and there, among her make-up and jewellery, I found her.

She was standing in front of the mirror puckering up as she applied her lipstick before reaching for her hairbrush. Chatting away, she turned her head this way and that, ensuring there wasn't a hair out of place, before taking time to decide which necklace was to be today's choice. Finally, she reached for her Estée and sprayed it behind both ears, the full stop in her morning preparations. Mum was synonymous with her perfume. I picked the bottle up and sprayed it on my wrists, dabbing a little behind the ears. Closing my eyes, I took a long, slow breath, and as she seeped through me I delighted in her presence once more, even if it was only for a short while.

Back in her bedroom the sun streamed in the window onto her bed. I sat down on the bed opposite hers, where we had taken turns sleeping in the weeks and days before. Picking up my phone, I searched for a photograph from just over a week ago, a sneaky shot I'd taken from the door without her knowing. Mum was sitting propped up in bed engrossed in *Dancing with the Stars* and Michael and Eileen were sitting on the bed I now sat on. If ever there was a moment that assured me Mum had made the right decision to stay at home, that photo showed it. Despite how unwell she was, she'd desperately wanted to watch the semi-final of the show that night but had shaken her head when I'd suggested we put it on in the television in her bedroom.

'No,' she'd said, 'watching television in my room would be a very bad habit to start.'

Thankfully, Michael had convinced her on this occasion that she should, and we had sat for a glorious couple of hours, listening as she criticised or praised the celebrity dancers, oblivious to our pain when we would hear her say, 'I'm so looking forward to the final next week.'

What a privilege that last week had been. To be able to sit by her side, morning and night, as her body slowly wound down. To be there in her waking, to listen to her worries and to take comfort in her complete acceptance of her dying.

'I'm happy,' she had said, more than once.

Looking around the room, I reflected that there were probably not too many people with a bedroom such as this, which held so many memories. The room and en-suite had been built by Dad years before, an extension onto the side of the house, incorporating the garage and extending our hallway. He had done most of the work himself, with a little help from the rest of us, or so old photos would imply. They show us as a family, decked out in shorts, T-shirts and wellies, mixing cement and putting up block walls, although I'm not too sure those photos speak the whole truth, as I can't imagine ten-year-old me was of much use. For a long time after Dad died, such memories had been lost to me. No matter how hard I tried I could only picture him broken by MND, unable to walk or talk, but thankfully as the years have passed my memory has rescued him. Sitting on the bed missing Mum, I smiled remembering those happy days.

Every chance Dad got he'd spent outside with his tools, a pencil always behind his ear. A talented carpenter, he loved nothing more than to be busy, building a new kitchen or improving the house by putting in our central heating by himself, building wardrobes or putting up shelves. We were accustomed to being woken by sawing or hammering at the earliest hour on the weekends, and as a young child I spent much of my time wandering after him like a puppy, 'helping' him hammer and sand small blocks of wood. However, I remember one occasion when I was forbidden from helping him, when the very bedroom I was sitting in now was once the garage, and within it the present he was making for me for Christmas.

I was seven years old and Dad was building me a doll's house. Each evening after work and on weekends he would disappear into the garage and I wasn't allowed follow him.

'It'll be a surprise,' he said.

Not being the most patient of children, I nearly burst waiting. When he wasn't working on it, my surprise sat hidden beneath a large blanket but I never dared venture in for a peep. Sometimes I'd stand outside the garage door, listening to Dad sawing or sanding, and wonder what exactly it might look like. But even in my imagination I could never picture it.

Finally, Christmas Day arrived. Growing up, we didn't get a lot of extras during the year but come Christmas, Mum and Dad pushed the boat out. On Christmas Eve night we hung a long piece of twine, like a makeshift clothesline, from one end of the kitchen to the other. On it we pegged up our largest pair of trousers for Santa to fill and placed a chair underneath in case there was an overflow! Come morning there were toys aplenty in our kitchen. Years later I asked Mum how she afforded such generosity and she said she began to save from the second week in January. As time has passed, those magical Christmases have merged one into another, but the year I got my doll's house has continued to have a place of its own, as I remember seeing it for the very first time.

It was almost three feet tall and three feet long. To a small-for-her-age seven-year-old, that was enormous. The front of the house was closed in, its walls decorated with white stipple paint just like our own house. There were three curtained windows on the top floor and two large ones on the bottom. However, it was when you turned the house around that the real wonder was revealed.

The other side was open. It had a central stairway of polished wood with a turn half-way up. Upstairs was a large bedroom and bathroom and downstairs a sizable sitting room and kitchen. There was also a small room under the stairs which could become a playroom. Mum had wallpapered the walls throughout and made chairs, a table and cupboards, using painted or covered matchboxes and cheese cartons, as well as little beds with tiny pillows, sheets and blankets.

It was far beyond anything I could have dreamed of. I spent hundreds of hours kneeling in front of it, imagining and playing out all manner of dramas for the many different lives I created for my dolls who lived within it. For years it stood in my bedroom, long after I'd finished playing with it, before finally moving to the attic. There it stayed for almost ten years until I gave birth to Aoife.

As she grew, I watched her develop the same love for dolls I once had, and when she was three years old my doll's house made the move from the home in which my dad had lovingly created it, to my home in Cork. It was a bitter-sweet day, with Dad not around to see the transfer from one generation to the next as he'd died six years earlier.

I am not sure which of us was more excited that day, as Aoife saw it for the first time and I saw it once again, after so many years. It was exactly as I'd remembered it, and she and I spent a lovely afternoon setting it up with furniture, dolls and small dogs. As a child, I had only ever found two dolls and a tiny dog to live in it, as most other dolls were too large. However, toys had changed a lot in the intervening years and my daughter already had tiny furniture and a great many small dolls, so even at three years of age she had a more sophisticated house with a larger family than I ever had.

For twenty years that doll's house remained central to our playroom, loved by my four children, by Jessica and Jennifer who I minded, by my godchildren and the many visitors who called to our home. I suspect Dad never imagined, as he was building it for me all those years before, that well into the future the little hands of his grandchildren would have played with it, lost in their far-away worlds of make-believe, a forever link with the Dad I knew and the grandfather they never had the good fortune to meet.

Sitting in Mum's bedroom surrounded by such memories, I was reluctant to return to the present. I felt weary, with a tiredness that had nothing to do with sleep and everything to do with sadness and grief for a life that had changed forever. I put my perfumed wrist to just beneath my nose, looking for a fresh shot of Mum. Her perfume had become challenged by the smell of fresh flowers in the room, as in the preceding week we'd filled it with lilies, white hydrangeas and freesia, the arrival of each bouquet bringing a smile to her face, even when she was too tired to speak. It would be impossible to remember Mum and not think of flowers and the garden, a love for which she passed on to all of us.

There was also a sense of relief the day after Mum's funeral, not that she had died but that she had got the ending she most wanted, peaceful and at home. However, as I went to bed after midnight that night I was exhausted with emotion and grief. While I could cope with her dying before what would have been a most difficult birthday, I couldn't be consoled as I faced the prospect of my first Mother's Day without her – and away from my own children.

I felt desperately sorry for myself. There was no need to keep my door open in case Mum called, my phone beside the bed in case she rang, or my dressing gown handy in case I had to get up in the night. It was after midnight; Mother's Day had officially begun. I pulled the duvet over me and curled up, letting my tears flow, but became distracted by something at my feet. I pulled back the covers and there was a card. *Mom* was written on the front. Opening it, I saw that it was a Mother's Day card from my eldest daughter, Aoife.

Aoife would never have expressed a love of English when she was in school, but this card was beautifully written, her words perfectly chosen. I read them over and over, and once the initial tears of gratitude and love had fallen, I began to feel stronger. I wasn't just Trish, the daughter who had lost her mother, I was Trish, the mother of Aoife, Tiarnán, Naoise and Caoimhe. A woman who had come a long way from the young mother who had held her first child twenty-eight years before. The young mother who had no idea of the difficulties she was about to face, difficulties that had little to do with the everyday trials of rearing a young child and everything to do with the man who had robbed her of her childhood.

The following morning I opened the other Mother's Day cards and presents my children had left for me the day before, devouring every word, their cards more heartfelt than usual. How I wished they were close enough to hug, imagining their noisy chatter as they vied for the honour of favourite child, while joking among themselves as to whose present was the most coveted and which one obviously wasn't.

I thought of Mum and her mothering. My childhood was in a different era, when being a stay-at-home mother was expected. I don't recall ever returning from school and Mum not being there, and lunch was always on the table. Each evening we had not only dinner but dessert, and tins in the kitchen were always full of home-made bread, cakes, buns and apple tart. Mum was the dominant parent, happy to leave Dad in the role of good cop to her bad, dealing with our misdemeanours herself rather than waiting for him to come home from work. At a time when children were routinely slapped, it was not part of my growing-up. If my early childhood were a feeling, it would be warmth and security.

During that first Mother's Day without Mum, I occasionally caught a glimpse of the reality of her loss, but mostly I was in a haze, remembering her with great fondness while not fully grasping that she was never coming back. Later that night, as

Eileen, Michael and I sat in the sitting room, we toasted Mum, re-telling many stories that showed her wicked sense of humour, some of which I had forgotten, others I'd heard regularly but never tired of. These stories were part of our family's oral history, stories with simple titles given to them which had us laughing out loud before the tale was even begun. Titles such as 'Billie Bunter under the Stairs', or 'The IRA Man and the Clothesline'. How we laughed as we remembered how much fun Mum was to be around, and as we laughed, we cried, remembering she was gone.

Yet, beneath the tears there was a large part of me grateful for those feelings of pain, sadness and loss. Grateful that I did so deeply mourn her, that our relationship had been strong enough to survive Gibney's abuse. Knowing that for a while it had come close to tearing us apart. For when I had first opened up to Mum about what had happened, after I had made two statements to the guards, it had not gone well.

17

The Gamble

In January 1993 I rang the number for Blackrock garda station, which Gary had included in his letter. I hadn't asked if others had done the same, afraid that if I discovered they had not, my resolve might falter. Having made the initial phone call, I withdrew into myself, trying to recall details of some of the assaults, preparing for when I would have to give a statement to the guards. Sitting alone, by day or night, I rewound the reel of memories, watching the film roll, as if it were not my life I was recalling but that of someone else. As my appointment neared I became ever more inward-looking, outwardly busy with my little one while beneath the surface preoccupied by my thoughts, unwilling to share them, not even with Eamonn.

In the loneliness of the night I lay awake, fearing that the holes in my memory would make me look ridiculous, my story a half truth, or that my testimony would be so scant that my charges might not even be considered. However, of all the things I worried and stressed over, my greatest dread was finding the words for what I had lived through and having to speak them aloud.

The day of my appointment dawned and, feeling nauseated, heart pounding, I travelled to Dublin alone and walked the familiar street in Blackrock village towards the Garda station. The push and pull, to go or not go, was intense. *Did I want to do this?* Yes, of that I had no doubt. *Could I do it?* Of that I was less sure. Outside the station I stopped, trying to picture what it was like inside.

Where would I be giving my statement? Would it be a male or female guard? Or both? I seriously regretted not letting Eamonn come with me. I'd seen how hard it had been for him to let me go alone but I knew I was stronger alone, fearing that if he were by my side, I would have been one hug away from falling apart. Slowly, I walked to the front door. I was twenty-six years old, a mother, a wife, a sister, a daughter, a victim. In a whisper, I told the guard on duty I had an appointment.

'And you are?' he said.

As he waited for my reply, I paused, aware that to answer him was to break my anonymity. There would be no going back.

'My name is Patricia McCahill,' I said. As I heard myself speak my name, loud and clear, I suddenly felt different – stronger, prouder and determined. I was going to nail Gibney.

Much of the details of that interview are lost to me. In the 1990s things were different to how they are now. In order to bring a prosecution, I needed to remember not only what Gibney had done to me but where the assault took place, in what year, on what date and at what time. This was hugely problematic to a girl who had very successfully buried those details out of reach. In order to get the best out of my statement, I was asked to return for a second interview, some weeks later. It is this interview I remember more clearly.

I dreaded going back, sick at the thought of returning to the station and reliving what Gibney had done to me. Once again, I went alone. For several hours, two extremely kind, sympathetic guards, one female, one male, teased out the details of my original statement, trying to get to the places I had not been able to go the first time around. Some assaults I could remember the details of, but not the where or when, others I remembered all too clearly but found them almost impossible to share. I remember the guards' empathy as they handed me a tissue for my tears. I recall them gently coaxing me to sit down when I snapped, shouting at them in rage that I was leaving. I remember them praising me as I drank a cup of tea, unable to look them in the eye knowing they had been writing every detail down. Finally, I remember sitting at the table as they read my statement back to me and my tears as I said, 'Yes, it is all true,' and signed it.

Leaving the station, there was no high that it was over, no relief at having told my story, but rather a crushing exhaustion and a chilling sense of foreboding, that this was the beginning of a whole new nightmare and my life was spinning out of my control.

In the days afterwards I was filled with anxiety. I had outed myself, but I wasn't ready for the effects of that act. Now the wheels of justice had been set in motion and there was no going back. I knew I had to tell Mum.

After weeks of fretting over when and how, Eamonn and I, along with baby Aoife, travelled to Dublin to visit 108 for the weekend. Instead of my usual delight at the trip home, I was full of dread, knowing the bomb I was about to drop.

I don't remember exactly the moment, or the

words I used, but I do remember where I was when I opened up to Mum. I stood in the kitchen, the heart of our home, as I told her Gibney had abused me, blurting it out as best I could, this dark secret that I had carried within me for so long. It was the hidden nightmare behind the actions of the moody, door-slamming teen, who felt anxious and alone. It was the secret I guarded closely when, at sixteen, my parents questioned my spending too much time with Gibney, ignorant to what was wrong, but picking up that something wasn't quite right. But how could I speak of the unspeakable? How could I tell them, with Gibney always there in the back of my mind, watching, listening, waiting to pounce?

Now, standing opposite Mum, I waited for her reaction, desperately wishing for her arms to open and take away the pain and confusion of those years. The clock ticked as a chasm opened up in the space between us, filled with the words we both should have said but couldn't.

It was beyond Mum's imaginings to

understand how a father of young children, a man she trusted, could be capable of the rape of a child. She had no such experience in her life that might have led her to understand what I was trying to tell her, and nothing she remembered in my growing up that would have helped her believe it was true.

And yet understanding was exactly what I expected of her, asking her to witness the most vulnerable place within me, to react in the moment to her broken child. But it was an impossible ask. My head began to spin as I watched her shocked reaction, her utter inability to take in my words. A feeling of sickness rose within me. *She didn't get it.*

She finally reacted when I told her I had gone to the guards. Instead of speaking words of concern at the toll the publicity and court case might have on me, on Eamonn, on my marriage, she entreated me to please reconsider, to think about what I was doing. My rage was intense and immediate, and under a hail of vicious words she quickly retreated to her bedroom. The door banged shut. Our discussion on Gibney was over.

I stormed out of 108, slamming the front door behind me as a tearful Eileen came after me, asking me to stay. Sitting in the passenger seat, I waited as Eamonn strapped Aoife into her seat and packed the car. As we drove away, I stared out the window, a part of me hoping to see Mum come to the door. But there was to be no last-minute appearance. I caught Eamonn's glance in my direction and saw the hurt he had for me in his eyes. Sitting in silence, my rage and hurt infused till I could not tell one from the other, I was grateful for the squeeze of Eamonn's hand, his quiet, unstinting support.

Mum and I had clashed before, but never on this scale. My temper is notoriously quick and short-lived, but during this period it simmered for months, boiling over at anyone or anything with the minimum of provocation. Decades later I can still remember the hurt, the anger and the sadness of that time, but I can also better imagine what it was like for Mum, to face such a nightmare reality, out of the blue, without Dad to help her through.

And while we did find a way back, it was through carefully plastering over the black hole of hidden hurts, anger and misunderstanding that lay between us. An outsider, witnessing our phone chats in the months and years afterwards, might have thought we shared a close bond, but in the background there was a wealth of conversations not had – about Gibney, the guards, the court case or how either of us was coping. As time ticked by and I waited for news of Gibney being charged, I yearned for our old closeness, and the easy chats that had been the way of things for so long, but were no more.

After what happened when I opened up to Mum, I struggled to tell anyone else. Breaking the silence of abuse is always difficult, but in the Ireland of the early 1990s, where shame and silence were the order of the day, there was even less of a roadmap than there is today. It was still a family tragedy if a girl became pregnant, homosexuality was only recently made legal, and child abuse was not spoken about. Finding the words to explain what had happened to me, without going into detail, was nearly impossible. What did I mean, Gibney abused me? Each person I told listened with their own understanding of what they imagined abuse to mean, and with their own idea of what they would have done. Painfully, I suspected most believed they would never have let it happen to them. Telling anyone was a gamble, not knowing how much they would empathise or understand. Sometimes I won, sometimes I lost.

There was the friend whose cloaked judgement echoed in my head for months afterwards. I hadn't needed to tell her, but she was a close friend, and I had wanted to. Leaving our house that evening, I hugged Eamonn for a little longer than usual as I said goodbye, summoning my courage.

In the intimate setting of a small restaurant, my friend had chatted freely, not witnessing my distraction, my stumbling as I tried to grasp the right moment to tell my story. As I finally spoke, awkwardly trying to find the right words, no hand reached across the table, no hurt showed behind her eyes. My heart sank. Face burning, I stopped speaking and we sat for what felt like an eternity before she responded: 'But surely you knew it was wrong?'

In that moment I wished more than anything I could turn back the minutes, unsay my words. She had said what I feared most people thought. What *my own mother* thought. *How could I have let it happen?*

Arriving home later that evening there was no need to fill Eamonn in on the details, a shake of my head sufficed. Her words haunted me. *Surely you knew it was wrong.* In the weeks since I'd given my garda statement, shame and guilt had coated my body with a layer of dirt I could feel but couldn't see. In the days after conversing with my friend, the urge to wash became more intense, even though I knew no amount of scrubbing would cleanse me.

One evening, not too long after, I sat to watch television, my skin stinging, red raw in places after my shower. Eamonn sat opposite, so close I could have reached out and touched him, but he might as well have been a million miles away. My mind was troubled, filled with thoughts I couldn't share, full of guilt for keeping them secret. *What was he thinking?* I wondered. *Did he miss the lively, fun-loving girl he'd fallen for?* I certainly did. It had been four months since Gary's letter had arrived, and in that time, everything had changed.

Curled up on the couch I felt old, broken, dirty. Thoughts of sneaking off for another shower began to nag me. *Would Eamonn notice?* Even as I wondered, I knew I was in trouble. If I didn't stop this washing now, I might never stop. I knew the dirt was all in my mind, but it felt so real that some days I even imagined there was a smell from me. And everything was intensifying. I knew it was now or maybe never. I made up my mind. I would stop.

So began a new battle. One day at a time I

fought that inner voice telling me I was unclean. I challenged myself to shower only once a day and wash my hands only when necessary. It was difficult to cook and feed my daughter with hands I imagined being dirty but gradually the feeling lessened, although even today I can remember what that coating of dirt felt like on my skin. However, although the sensation lessened, I was still very fragile, supersensitive to the comments of friends or family.

During that time, Eamonn was my only constant. He never asked questions or pressed me to share how I was feeling. It was not his way to seek to heal me but rather to just be there, knowing when to walk away with just a gentle squeeze of my hand or when to hold me. I didn't share my everyday battles with him, and he never pushed me to, but I knew he was there, ready and waiting for whenever I needed him.

The decision to tell a friend was a momentous one, and when they hugged and supported me I sighed with relief. However, telling family that

I'd been abused for many years, by a man they knew, was a seismic event and the repercussions were enormous, as each family member struggled to realise that the moody teenager they once knew was not who they thought she was, and that the shared life they remembered bore little resemblance to my reality. Like my closest friends, their reactions were important to me and went a long way towards my healing, or not.

Initially my sisters, Doris and Caroline, were incensed at Gibney, as was my brother-in-law. They relentlessly pursued him, fighting to have him excluded from the pool and going to the court in my name. It meant the world to me that they were fighting on my behalf. However, even knowing I had their support, there were still times when I felt very much alone.

Mum and I were trying to navigate our new norm but Gibney was the elephant in the room, never openly discussed within the walls of 108. Perhaps at family gatherings everyone was mindful of upsetting me, or Mum, but much of the time there was no talk about him or what had happened. The unspeakable nature of all that I had revealed weighed heavily in the atmosphere, as did the burden of my shameful, secret past, like dirty linen hung out to dry.

One afternoon, having travelled to Dublin, I arranged to meet my older brother, Ben. We'd had almost no time to chat since I'd gone to the guards and I'd no idea how much he knew about my story, or what he thought of it. At the time, I was in the midst of my attempts to break the cycle of constant showering, and was struggling badly with the nightmares and flashbacks.

Ben had recently rented a house in Sandycove near Dún Laoghaire, so I'd arranged to meet him near the seafront. Tearful and nervous, I arrived, ready to put my heart in his hands. *What if he rejected me?* Ben wasn't the most demonstrative of people at the best of times, not one to use two words when one would do. But being my big brother, I desperately wanted his support.

It was a warm day, but the sea breeze carried a chill. I was early. Sitting on a bench, I looked out to sea, towards Dún Laoghaire pier. How often

I had walked it as a teenager and young adult, listening to the sails and masts tinging off one another, my head full of ideas of learning to sail … and escape. My heart was beating overtime as I waited.

Lost in thought, Ben's arrival caught me by surprise. He didn't speak, but stood in front of me, his arms open wide. I stepped into them and he enfolded me. I held onto him tightly, afraid to let a tear fall, but struggling to hold them back while he squeezed me in his embrace. As our hug ended, he stepped away and I saw he was holding a single red rose. Leaning forward, he kissed my cheek and whispered in my ear, 'This is for you, my beautiful, brave sister.'

Driving home that afternoon, I was a lot less broken. Being believed and supported in such a way empowered me.

But if I thought the worst was over, I was way off the mark. For in truth, the nightmare had barely begun.

18

Awaiting
Judgement Day

During those months of 1993 as I waited for
Gibney to be charged, life was hard, every day a
mental and emotional battlefield. I tried to remain
strong by imagining what lay in store for him,
picturing his face on discovering his victims had
come forward. Would he be arrested or brought
in for questioning? Would he be surprised or
angry? Might he even feel guilty? A part of me
thrilled as I pictured his fall from grace. With

such imaginings, though, came the inevitable slap
of reality: some day in the future I would have to
face him, to find the words to tell in court what
he had done and possibly fight to prove it. The
thought terrified me, but even more daunting
was the possibility of my secret being outed in the
newspapers, of everyone knowing what Gibney
had done to me. I was not ready to go public.

George Gibney was quite the personality in the
Ireland of the 1980s and early '90s. It was not
unusual for him to feature in newspaper stories,
with pictures of him meeting politicians and
highly connected businesspeople as he advocated
for Ireland's first fifty-metre swimming pool. He
had a high public profile as coach to European
Championship silver medallist Gary O'Toole,
and to the Irish swim team in the Los Angeles
Olympics in 1984 and Seoul Olympics in 1988. In
the year before I'd gone to the guards he had been
on television as studio analyst for the Barcelona
Olympics. I knew it was unlikely that the fall from
grace of such a high-profile personality would go

unnoticed, but it didn't stop me hoping that I could avoid being linked publicly to the case.

On 6 April that year, three months after I walked into Blackrock garda station in Dublin, Gibney appeared in court *on seventeen charges relating to four females and one male*. I knew by the dates they were not my charges, but the process had begun. That day was a strange one as I tried to stay busy tackling mundane tasks such as washing and ironing while images of Gibney appearing in court played in my mind. The inner dialogue was exhausting.

Serves you right, you fecker, I shouted from my imagined spot in the public gallery.

Oh my God, what have I done? I despaired, sitting at the kitchen table.

My two sisters went to the court that day, but the case was over by the time they arrived. They told me, however, that as Gibney left, the car in which he was a back-seat passenger, driven by his solicitor, crashed just outside the courthouse, much to the delight of the waiting press. Imagining that scene made me smile. But as I hung up, I processed their words: 'much to the delight of the waiting press'. *Did that mean it would be in the papers? Would he be named?*

After a sleepless night I scanned the morning papers and spotted a small, easy to miss two-inch column on page two of one of them.

Sportsman charged

The article was just the bare facts of the charges, noting that the 'senior sporting figure' could not be named. I read it many times, relieved that he wasn't identified and that it was not big news.

'It's in another paper too,' said Eamonn, pushing the publication in my direction. My heart sank; I knew by the tone of his voice that this article was different.

Man faces list of 17 charges

I took a few deep breaths as I read this larger piece, on page seven.

'The detective Charlie Byrne had met the accused by appointment at Blackrock garda station that morning.'

I let myself imagine Gibney driving to the garda station. Had someone given him a lift? What had he told them?

'He took him into custody on foot of a warrant.'

My heart quickened as I imagined Gibney being cautioned and seventeen charges read out to him. The dates were from 1967, the year after I was born, to 1979, the year I joined Trojan. That meant Gibney had been nineteen when he assaulted his first child. He had continued to abuse children for twenty-six years.

The article went on: *'The public gallery was packed, with some of the victims and their relatives present.'* I thought of the families of those I knew who were there. Unlike the survivors who went, I knew that even if I had been in Dublin I could not have gone – I was not ready to go public.

One week later the case was in court again.

Sportsman bailed on sex charges

The words 'sex charges' made me cringe. How was it correct to refer to the assaults Gibney had perpetuated on young children as 'sex'?

The article said that a judge *'was refusing to deal with the indecency charges in the District Court and the representative of the DPP said they would come before the Circuit Court'*. What did that mean? Was it round one to us? Where was the Circuit Court? Wherever it was, the thought of going there terrified me. Yet there was a part of me cheering, *We will nail that bastard.*

One month later, the detective rang with the news I'd been waiting for: Gibney had been charged with some of my accusations, more were to follow.

'He seemed shocked when he heard your name,' he said.

Hanging up, I sat on the floor beside the phone, digesting his words. Why was I so stunned? It wasn't as if I didn't know this was coming. Fear gripped me as I recalled the detective's words: *He seemed shocked when he heard your name.* Gibney knew I had come forward. Even after all this time, I was still afraid of him.

On Tuesday, 18 May, six weeks after his first

court appearance, I read that Gibney had been charged with the first of my accusations.

Indecency case bail

'A leading sports personality was charged with five more offences,' the two-inch column read. I re-read it over and over. It was done. But was this it? Five charges! Indecent assault? *Was that really the name for what he had done to us?* Five charges, for all those years of abuse? Was the agony of going to the guards, the estrangement from Mum ... was it all worth it, for this?

I wondered how many would read the paper that day and skim over the column, never imagining the hurt and changed lives behind those few words, the courage it had taken to go to the guards or the tsunami it had caused within the family. Reading it for the hundredth time, I noticed it didn't say if the charges were brought against him by one or two people, but I knew it was possibly two of us, as I had been in touch with another girl who was interviewed around the same time as myself. I was grateful that day to be in her company on the page. She could have remained silent, but she didn't. It was as if we were facing Gibney together and despite my distress, that day I felt a lot less alone than I might have.

Once Gibney had been charged, I slowly began to relax, immersing myself in family life and doing what I did best ... forgetting. Eamonn, Aoife and I went to Portugal for a week and it was there I gave Eamonn the brighter news that I'd kept quiet during those turbulent days: I was pregnant again. It was exactly what we needed, and as he placed his hands protectively over my belly, I smiled. This was a future I was willing to imagine, beyond any court case or questioning. February 1994, the expected arrival of baby number two.

Despite my all-day nausea, I arrived home from the holiday with a secret smile. It was too early to tell anyone, but I felt happier than I had done for a long time. The thought of my new baby filled me with a strength I'd forgotten I possessed.

Gibney and the court case had no place in my thoughts. Life was simple again, shrinking to within the walls of my home, being with Eamonn, caring for Aoife and coping with the trials of early pregnancy.

Eight or nine weeks in, I woke one day feeling different. I ate breakfast and waited for the nausea to strike. Perhaps it was just nature's way of giving me a break, I thought, helping me recover from days and nights of sickness. But I couldn't shake my unease. As the morning ended, the cramps began. Not long after, I began to bleed.

Two days and two scans later I lay in the ultrasound room of the Bon Secours Maternity Hospital, Cork, Eamonn and I staring at a screen, holding our breath for sight or sound of our little one's beating heart. We saw the result in the doctor's face before he spoke.

I had gone to the hospital believing I would be strong enough to cope whatever the outcome, that I had not yet bonded with this tiny being. But I was wrong. His words hit like gunshot, peppering my body as I sat up and cleaned the gel from my empty belly. 'I'm really sorry, there is no heartbeat.'

Our little one was gone. I'd spent weeks conversing with it, wondering at its sex, imagining it playing with its sister, even its first day at school. Instead I was to go to theatre, with barely any time to hold Eamonn and share our pain, to cry our hearts out, to mourn. As I waited for the anaesthetist to put me to sleep for a D and C, I placed my hands on my empty stomach and whispered goodbye to my little one and the future it would never see.

'Miscarriage,' the doctor had said, 'ends one in four pregnancies.' *Was that supposed to make me feel better or worse?* In the days afterwards, I found it difficult to share my feelings of loss with Eamonn, believing he had barely known the baby was there. I didn't cry when he was around and we didn't speak about it, but I could sense the sadness between us. Then one evening he said, 'I know you are not one for religion, but I thought it would be nice to go to the church and light a candle together.'

Immediately, I knew this was what I needed, a moment with Eamonn to acknowledge our baby and to say goodbye. With Aoife happy to 'help' us light the candle, we placed it in the centre of the altar, and as Eamonn slipped his hand into mine in the quietness of the church we said a silent goodbye to Dara, a name we chose for our baby which would encompass either gender. It would be many weeks before I would come to terms with the realisation that there was no baby, and for even longer I mourned the child few even knew I had lost.

Yet, hand in hand with my grief, life ticked along, and towards the end of June, I got a phone call from the detective leading our case, informing me that Gibney had been charged with the rest of my accusations, a further five charges. With a total of twenty-seven charges against him, our case was now complete.

19

Missing Years

The court case was scheduled for October but within weeks we heard Gibney was appealing the charges and when October came, we learned he was going to the High Court to have them dismissed, due to the length of time between alleged crimes and charges. 'Such an appeal is only time-wasting,' we were assured, but I was not convinced; the Gibney I knew had connections everywhere and could, I felt, get out of anything.

In October the High Court rejected his appeal, but he further appealed to the Supreme Court. More time-wasting we were told, but again I wondered.

During this time I grew weary, juggling an outwardly happy life alongside the ongoing flashbacks, nightmares and worries about the court case, as well as the monthly disappointment of no new pregnancy. Just before Christmas, we heard that the Supreme Court was allowing Gibney's appeal for a judicial review in the High Court. We had come full circle and were facing into the New Year no nearer to justice.

Yet there was hope. Just weeks into January, six months after my miscarriage, I discovered I was pregnant. So great was my delight – and trepidation – that I spent half a mortgage on pregnancy tests, just to be sure. Although I was nervous that I might miscarry, I didn't dwell on it, daring to believe this little one was here to stay. As January turned to February, I felt my world brighten. A year had passed since I had first gone to the guards and while the court case continued to be a dark cloud on my horizon, cocooned in my pregnancy I lived in the now, doing my best to forget about Gibney, the court case and the ensuing publicity it would bring.

Unfortunately, my tactic of forgetting was not holding as strong as before. As my pregnancy progressed, the flashbacks and nightmares intensified, triggering painful memories. As my bump grew, so too did my sense of vulnerability, the uncertainty of my future playing on my mind. *Would I have to go to court before the baby was born? Would the press be there?* And most terrifying of all, *Would I be able to remember all that I must?*

Sixteen months had passed since I'd given the guards my initial statement and, even when I tried, I found it impossible to remember what was in it. I could only imagine that with such pathetic recall I'd be thrown out of court, my charges swiftly dismissed. Such fears were particularly present at night, and alongside them was a fresh set of troubles. The dirt was back, coating my body just as it had the year before. As I once again fought the urge to excessively wash my hands and shower, I retreated into myself, unable to tell Eamonn, or anyone, I needed help.

Approximately five months into my pregnancy I went to my GP for a routine visit. Fear and anxiety were taking their toll on my everyday life. While outwardly I smiled and chatted, daily tasks were a struggle, my mind so preoccupied that I wandered car parks wondering on which level I'd parked the car, and zoned out of conversations as sounds and images of the past invaded my senses. We were still waiting to hear what the High Court would decide, but having rejected Gibney's appeal once, I remained hopeful. Physically and emotionally exhausted, I sat opposite my GP and smiled a cheery hello. As a matter of routine, he asked how I was.

I formed the words to tell him I was fine, that all was good in my world, but instead I heard myself say that I was not. He sat and listened as I quietly told him I had been abused. I didn't cry, nor did my voice shake. I didn't tell him any details, nor did he ask. Finally, I said, 'And now I've to go to court, but I'm really struggling to remember all that I must.'

His face showed no emotion as he sat for a moment considering what I'd told him. I wished the ground would open, regret flooding through me. *Why had I said anything? I didn't want his help.*

'Would you consider counselling as a way to unlock the past?' he gently suggested.

I imagined a heavy shutter slowly begin to descend between us. How tempting to let it fall and lock myself behind it, away from his prying eyes, talk of prosecutors and conversations such as this. To go back, to before I'd told him, to before Gary's letter, to my normal life *before*.

Counselling? Really? I couldn't even tell Eamonn what I was feeling, how could I tell a stranger? Sitting in silence, my kindly GP waited for a reply.

'I don't think I want to remember,' I whispered, 'and I don't think I could tell anyone if I did.'

Another silence fell as my face burned with shame and guilt, wondering if he could imagine what I was holding back. *Had he any idea what Gibney had done to me?* Finally, in a matter-of-fact voice he said, 'But you're going to go to court. You will be questioned, and you'll need to be able to remember.'

I knew he was right, but hearing him say it was terrifying. I'd watched so many movies where witnesses had been ripped apart. *Would it be like that? But what was the alternative? To let Gibney get away with it because of holes in my remembering?* A wave of anger washed over me. No chance.

So I took the name of a woman counsellor he thought would be a good match for me, and as soon as I got home, I made an appointment.

A couple of weeks later I stood in the hall of my friend Olive's house, the same friend who'd taken Gary's letter from me eighteen months before. Olive was one of a handful who knew my secret and she looked every bit as nervous as I felt. Saying goodbye to almost three-year-old

Aoife and Jessica, the little one I minded, I smiled as they lined up for a kiss, anxious to get to the playroom. They skipped off, blissfully oblivious to the charged atmosphere in the narrow hall. My friend reached to embrace me, but I backed off, all too aware I was one hug away from crumbling.

'Good luck,' she said.

'Thanks,' I replied, and left.

Half an hour later I was standing outside the counsellor's door. To this day I cannot see her face or tell you how old she was, but in my mind she was softly spoken and there was a warmth and kindness about her. I, on the other hand, was a hostile witness, there not by choice but by necessity. On that first visit she did her best to put me at ease, asking questions about where I was from, my marriage and home life. However, watching her take notes, every muscle within me clenched, as I waited for the elephant in the room to be addressed. And as I waited, I knew beyond all doubt I wasn't ready.

Many people speak highly of counselling,

how it was a lifeline thrown to them in a time of great despair, but for me it was a weekly hour of hell. I think of myself as a polite individual, but sitting there, week after week, I was reminded of my rebellious teenage self, reporting to the principal's office for some misdemeanour or other and refusing to co-operate with questioning. Ever the professional, my kindly counsellor battled on.

'Do you think you could write down what you see in your flashbacks?'

'Eh, no. I don't think so.'

'How about if you wrote it down and then burned it?'

'No.'

'Could you describe how you feel after one of your nightmares?'

'Sorry, no.'

'Could you remember where you were the first time you were abused?'

'No, definitely not!'

It wasn't that I didn't want to do what she asked, but even her asking was almost tipping me over the edge. The more she prodded, the more I feared losing control. It was bad enough that Gibney was bursting into my every day without invitation. Surely no one thought I should meet him in my memory by choice.

I was close to giving up when one day she asked if I had any old photos at home. I told her I had loads.

'Bring them in next week and we can look at them,' she said. 'Using them might help us talk.'

'How many do you want me to bring in?' I asked.

'As many as you like.'

I had a real skip to my step leaving her office that day. After weeks of non-co-operation, I was finally able to do something I'd been asked. *Was this progress?* I searched through the mountains of photos I had in boxes and albums and selected an overview of my life. Happy with my selection, I knocked at her door a week later, box of photos in hand, eager to show her I wasn't a hopeless case.

In her office was a large table. I scattered the

photos about it and left them as they landed, in no particular order. I was triumphant looking at my life on the table, from early tiny black-and-white photos of childhood, right up to a recent picture of my husband, daughter and me. I eagerly explained each photo, talking freely for the first time in weeks. Finally I stopped talking and waited, expecting her to ask questions, quiz me on my parents and siblings, query where some of the photos were taken and what age I'd been. But she remained silent.

'Are these all the photos you brought in?' she said eventually.

'Yes,' I replied.

'Did you leave any at home you thought about bringing in, but didn't?'

'No.'

She picked up two photographs. 'Tell me about these two,' she said.

'That first one,' I said, looking at a smiling younger me standing with a fellow swimmer, 'was when I was thirteen. We were on an international swim trip to Newcastle. It was the summer just before I joined Trojan Swimming Club.'

'And this one?' she said, handing me the other photo of a beaming me as I stood hand in hand with a young man.

I smiled. 'This is a photo of my husband, Eamonn, and me. We'd just met weeks earlier while on holiday in Cyprus and that is the first photo of us taken here in Ireland. I was nineteen.'

'Really?' she said.

As she paused, I wondered at the meaning behind her '*Really?*'

'And if you look at all the photos you've brought in today, do you notice anything?'

I looked at the forty or more photos littering the table, trying to view them through her eyes, but I could see nothing of note.

'No,' I said, giving up.

She held up the two photos again. 'This here, you tell me, is when you were thirteen. And this other one, you tell me, is when you were nineteen.'

I nodded.

'Well, look at all the photos on the table. Can

you see any of you between the ages of thirteen and nineteen?'

I was a little stunned. Surely she was wrong? Somewhere on that table there must be a photo of fifteen- or sixteen-year-old me? But after much checking, I had to admit there were none. I shook my head in disbelief.

'So,' she said, 'you made a choice today to not bring in any photos of your teenage years.'

'But I didn't choose not to,' I said, still scouring the table for proof she was wrong.

'I know you didn't, but at some level you did. Have you other photos at home?'

I didn't know, but leaving her office that day I sure was curious to find out. As soon as I got the chance later that evening, I pulled out every photo album and box of photos I possessed, searching for the teenager my mind was trying to erase. Sitting there, surrounded by what I'd thought was a lifetime of memories, I couldn't find her. *Was I going crazy? What did it mean?*

Returning to the counsellor a week later, she explained that those two photos pinpointed key moments in my life, one the end of *before* and the other the beginning of *after*, bookending the dark years in my life, my forgetting. The memories were all there, she assured me, but she was cautious about my digging too deeply, too quickly, especially while pregnant.

'You have built strong walls,' she said, 'only you can knock them down.'

I knew she was right. I had hoped she would not only magically unlock my memories, but having done so would rid me of them and the hurting, guilt and shame they brought with them. But of course I was the only one who could do that, and I had to be ready. As we said our goodbyes she wished me luck, both of us knowing I would not be back. I had built those walls to protect myself, and I was once again hiding behind them to keep both myself and my baby safe. Perhaps when I faced Gibney in court I would knock them down and let others see some of the horror behind them. Perhaps.

20

A Criminal
Walks Free

On 21 July 1994 I was twenty-eight years old
and thirty-four weeks pregnant when the final
phone call about our case came. The detective,
who had put so much into it, didn't beat around
the bush. He was sorry, the High Court decision
had not gone our way. As three-year-old Aoife
and her two friends played around me in the hall,
I zoned in and out, stunned, as he talked on. *The
dates were non-specific... They agreed the length of*

*time elapsed was too great… Impossible for him to
provide a defence… I'm so sorry…'*

I hung up, without a word of thanks to that
detective for all his work, not caring one jot how
difficult it must have been for him to pick up the
phone and ring me with that news. Picking my
way over scattered toys, I moved on auto-pilot to
the kitchen to make dinner.

I felt nothing – no upset, disappointment,
anger or hurt. *I knew he'd get out of it, the
bastard*, I thought. As the minutes ticked by, the
detective's words echoed in my head, louder and
louder. Each time I heard them they became a
little clearer, until it hit home. I didn't need to be
in court to imagine his grinning face, his smug
expression or his statement of denial. Gibney had
won.

Banging cups and plates, I set the table,
struggling to contain my rage. *Why had I been so
stupid? He was always going to win.*

On hearing Eamonn's key in the door later
that evening, the children ran to greet him as I

took a deep breath and fixed my bravest face. For a moment, everything was as it should have been, Aoife dancing a welcome to her dad with her two friends joining in, their delight in his arrival loud and enthusiastic. I stood watching, putting off the moment when I would have to admit Gibney's victory out loud, but as Eamonn leaned towards me for our usual welcome home kiss, tears spilled down my face.

'It's over,' I whispered. 'Gibney won.'

Saying the words out loud was so much more wounding than the whispered voice in my head all afternoon. Eamonn reached to embrace me but I pushed him away, consumed by the feelings of anger, hurt and grief churning inside me. *Gibney had won.* The words stabbed at me, the pain of my defeat intense as I ran upstairs to the sanctuary of the bedroom. Curling up on the bed, as much as my bump would allow, I pushed my face into the pillow to stifle the sound of my sobs. My emotions ebbed and flowed as my tears fell: anger, at the last wasted eighteen months; despair, for ever believing we might find justice; and sorrow, for the young teenager who had bared her soul in finally telling her secret – only to face the ultimate defeat.

Eamonn came up to check on me but I needed to be alone and he quietly left. It took a while, but eventually the tears subsided. I caught sight of my red blotchy face in the mirror. *You're some eejit. What's the point in crying? It's over.* I turned to look at myself from the side. My bump by this time was enormous, bigger than in my first pregnancy. I placed my hands on my belly, feeling what I suspected to be a little foot sticking out, and a powerful sense of protectiveness came over me. *Feck Gibney.* Taking a deep breath, I opened the bedroom door and went downstairs. Aoife's friends had gone home, and it was nearly her bedtime, and I could hear her chattering to Eamonn as he put on her pyjamas. I joined them, nodding that I was okay in reply to Eamonn's questioning look. Eamonn took Aoife up to bed and as I went up to tuck her in she gently placed a kiss on my bump.

As she whispered goodnight to her future sibling I thought, *This is all that truly matters, my two little ones and Eamonn. Gibney can go to hell.*

Over the following weeks I did my best to pick up my life and forget, but my moods swung within a moment between acceptance and rage. *At least it was finally over ... I didn't have to go to court ... But Gibney was still coaching, in the high-profile Scottish swimming club, Warrender ... The court had let him off.*

My nightmares returned with a vengeance, and as I lay in the darkness, afraid to return to sleep, I was haunted by memories of the thirteen-year-old girl on the blocks; the fifteen-year-old swimmer who had earlier been raped in the toilets; the overnight babysitter of Gibney's children, afraid to go to sleep, awaiting the terrifying turn of the door handle in the middle of the night, knowing what was in store. Regardless of whether or not Gibney was ever tried in a court of law, his crimes were indelibly imprinted on my mind. I would forever remember what he had done, even if the courts decided it was too long ago to expect him to remember such events.

Six weeks after our case was struck out, I gave birth to my son, his arrival the most glorious distraction possible. Being a mother for a second time, I worried less and enjoyed the experience more. While Aoife's birth, three years before, had triggered hidden memories, Tiarnán's, for a while, assuaged them. I immersed myself in my young family and mostly forgot the past two years, relishing the early days of his life, with no threat of court hanging over me. It was over. It now fell to me to forget the past and build a better future.

21

Exposed

Days later, the phone rang. It was a call that would make a seismic difference to that imagined future.

'Hello,' a softly spoken voice said, 'my name is Johnny Watterson. I'm looking to speak with Patricia.'

Sitting on the floor of my hall, the phone held to one ear as I breastfed my six-week-old baby, I listened to Johnny's quiet, gentle voice as he spoke of Gibney and the injustice of the court's decision.

'I'm a journalist with the *Sunday Tribune*,' he explained. 'I would like to tell your stories and I intend to name George Gibney in the paper.'

I tried to digest what I had heard but was too shocked, wondering how a journalist had got my number. Gary, maybe? Johnny spoke at length, explaining that he had been following the case for a long time. He felt the court decision had been unfair and that it was wrong that Gibney was allowed continue to coach young children. I could barely take in what he was saying, still unable to process the thought that a journalist had found me.

'You will be anonymous,' he assured me. 'We will keep your name out of the paper.'

'What if he sues?' I asked.

'Then you might get your day in court after all,' he replied.

I promised I'd think about it and hung up. The idea of Gibney being named in the paper was both thrilling and terrifying. Yet I couldn't see it happening. Surely a newspaper couldn't name and accuse him when he had not been found guilty in court? When Eamonn came home I told him about Johnny's call; he too wondered if it were possible, but even the thought of it made us both smile.

'Do you think you would put your story in the paper?' Eamonn asked.

'No way,' I replied immediately. But as the night wore on, I wondered, could I?

Days passed, busy days with a house full of small children and a baby, but I couldn't stop thinking about it. Accepting that Gibney had got away scot-free was becoming more difficult, not less. Maybe going to the newspaper would work? Maybe this was the way the world would find out who the real George Gibney was? But I hadn't told most of my friends my story; how would I cope with them, or anyone else, reading it in a newspaper?

A few days later, Johnny rang again. Although I still had not decided what to do, the internal voice that raged at the lack of justice was becoming very vocal, and as Johnny told me that some of the other victims had agreed to let him tell their stories, it only got louder. When he asked if I had thought any further about telling mine, I didn't say that I had thought about nothing else.

'Will I definitely be anonymous?' I asked.

'Yes,' he said, 'you will all have fictitious names.'

Johnny continued to speak, about the article, his editor Peter Murtagh and all they were doing in order to satisfy their legal team. His passion for the story was obvious, yet I didn't feel like he was pursuing it for the glory of just another story but rather that he was doing it for us, Gibney's victims. Listening, I had no doubt that he was going to publish this story with or without me, but I could see that my thoughts and feelings mattered to him. That reassurance, along with the sincerity in his quiet voice and the fact I felt no pressure to take part, convinced me to trust him.

'I'll do it,' I said, surprising myself.

'I'll need you to allow me access your garda statement. That way I don't need to ask you any questions.'

I sat, taking in what he was saying. *Give him permission to access my statement ... to read it ... to know the intimate details of the assaults?* In the nearly two years since making my statement, I had never told anyone, not even Eamonn, a single detail of what George Gibney had done to me.

'Will you be printing the statements, or parts of them?' I asked, the image of my words appearing in the paper too sickening to imagine.

'We will probably print parts of them.'

The reality of what I was agreeing to do hit home, but my mind was made up.

'Okay,' I said, 'I'll do it.'

I hung up, the content of the call so at odds with my surroundings. I pressed pause on life for a moment, staying where I was, sitting on the floor with six-week-old Tiarnán asleep in my arms as three-year-old Aoife and Jessica played with their dolls beside me. I supressed a sudden urge to gather them to me, enfold them and hold them close. How could anyone hurt a child? A smile spread across Tiarnán's face as he slept, and I felt an intense sadness for the child I had once been and the innocence Gibney had taken from me. *But go public? What about Mum? The family? Eamonn?* My face reddened at the thought of any of them reading my statement. *Was Johnny just a sensationalist?* Yet even as I worried, I knew that without the details in our statements, readers would never be able to imagine or believe what Gibney was guilty of. Later that night, after Aoife had gone to bed, I told Eamonn of my decision.

'What do you think?'

'Do whatever you have to do,' he said, without hesitation.

I can't remember the fine details of how we organised for my statement to be released from the guards to Johnny, but within weeks he had it in his possession. In the meantime, life was busy, with little time to dwell on what I had agreed to, or what might be going on in the offices of the *Sunday Tribune* in Dublin. Until one day in November, the phone rang, and my heart sank as I heard Johnny's distinctive voice on the other end. I waited, as he politely inquired into my well-being, all the time wondering, was this it?

Was he ringing to tell me when it was to be in the paper?

'Our legal team have looked at everything,' he said, 'and they've decided they need each of you to sign an affidavit, to prove that it is your statement and that everything in it is true.'

Relief flooded my body. More red tape meant the article would be delayed, and that suited me just fine. I don't remember the ins and outs of it, but I know that by Wednesday, 30 November, all our statements and affidavits were signed and had been received by the *Sunday Tribune*. Everything the legal team had asked for had been provided. There would be no more delays. The story was to be printed in four days' time, Sunday, 4 December 1994, just one month shy of the two-year anniversary of my first going to the guards.

I felt physically sick in the days before the article ran, unable to eat or sleep as Sunday raced towards us. The rest of my family knew about the upcoming story, but there was no discussion around it. What would Mum think? Or the others? I was torn, my conviction that I was making one of the biggest mistakes of my life only outweighed by my determination to see it through. On the Saturday, my brother Ben arrived with his wife and children to stay the night. He'd missed any signs of what had happened to me growing up and was determined to be there for me now.

'What if I can't face you tomorrow?' I said.

'That's okay,' he said, 'I just want to be here.'

That Sunday morning, I woke early, as Eamonn tip-toed out of the room. I lay in bed as my stomach cramped, imagining people all over the country already reading the paper. I heard the click of the front door closing, and the car starting up as Eamonn left for the shop. Tiarnán stirred in his tiny cot beside the bed. It had been made by Dad for my sister's dolls almost forty years before. Two snow-white, lace-edged curtains, made by Mum, covered both sides. I watched Tiarnán squirming as he blinked awake, his head turning in search of breakfast. I reached for him and he snuggled in, closing his eyes as he greedily fed. How simple his life was. He was quickly satisfied, and as I lay him back into his cot I wondered if Eamonn had got the paper yet. I'd asked him not to read it before I did. Would he? If I were in his shoes, I knew I certainly would. *Maybe it won't be as bad as I think?* Half an hour later, I heard the front door open. Sitting up, I took a deep breath. I would never again live in a time before the *Sunday Tribune* exposé. This was it. I was ready. But as Eamonn opened the bedroom door it was impossible to miss the look of hurt and sadness on his face.

'I didn't read it,' he said, handing me the folded-up newspaper.

I unfolded it. Gibney looked back at me, a photograph of his face taking up almost half the front page.

Top swim coach Gibney is child sex abuser

I immediately folded it up again, recoiling in horror, unable to unsee him, or the words, *'Gibney is child sex abuser'*. The statement of simple fact was so hard-hitting it left me winded. They believed us. I burst into tears, turning to hide my face in the pillow. Relief poured from me as Eamonn sat silently beside me, gently stroking my hair.

'Will I take it away?' he said, after a while.

My face didn't lift from the pillow as I shook my head. Gently kissing my hair, he said, 'I'll leave you for a little while. Will I take Tiarnán?'

'Yes, thanks. I've fed him already,' I said, not looking up.

As the door closed, I sat up. In panic I looked at the folded newspaper on the bed beside me. Even with it closed I was unnerved, remembering Gibney's face. *It's only a photo*. But it looked so lifelike, so real: his glasses, his beard, a pair of stopwatches around his neck. It was as if by opening it I feared he would magically appear in the room. Looking around, I spotted a large book on my locker. That would do. Taking it in one hand, I unfolded the paper and quickly covered the photograph before I had a chance to see it properly. I closed my eyes once more and took a

few breaths, slowly in ... out ... *You can do this.*
Opening them, I quickly scanned what was in
front of me. The story took up most of the front
page!

Molested children in Newpark, Glenalbyn
Victims' graphic details in sworn statements

I read the headings several times, letting them
sink in, the words *'victims' graphic details'* churning
my stomach. I couldn't bring myself to read
beneath the headings and once again lay back,
staring at the ceiling, digesting what I'd seen and
read. However, after a few minutes I felt better,
more ready, and began to read, starting with the
least upsetting heading.

'We must stop this man now'

Beneath it was a headshot of Gary, the article
a comment piece from him. It was obvious from
the writing that he was furious the courts had
accepted Gibney's appeal and that he had not been
tried and punished for his crimes. I felt a rush of
gratitude towards my childhood pal, remembering
the friendship he and I had shared and how

Gibney had ripped it apart. As a young boy, Gary had no idea of the truth behind our friendship ending, yet here he was, almost fifteen years later, doing all he couldn't do back then to make things better. Over the previous two years, while the case was going through the courts and I was in hiding, Gary had relentlessly pursued Gibney, alerting officials within swimming and speaking out as much as possible, but his concerns had fallen on deaf ears. Now he was joining Johnny in going public, bypassing those who refused to listen and telling everyone what Gibney was guilty of. After years of hiding, it was strange, but wonderful to know that someone was speaking up for me and for my fellow survivors.

Feeling braver, I read beneath the other headings: *The most successful coach in Irish swimming is a child sex abuser whose crimes date back almost thirty years, according to a number of former swimmers who have given sworn statements detailing his conduct.*

The fact that there were '*a number of former*

swimmers' gave me comfort. That I wasn't the only one who'd been abused made things less harrowing, somehow, and here we were, coming back at him.

'Mr Gibney denies the allegations vigorously and claims he is the victim of jealous rivals.'

A victim!

'"I am innocent of all the allegations that have been made against me. I know that I will always be guilty in the eyes of some, but I am innocent."'

I knew he would deny it, but reading him declare that he was 'innocent' was a blow to the stomach.

'As recently as last Thursday he was coaching children at a Scottish swimming club in Edinburgh,' the article continued. *'And this weekend he has been coaching the Scottish National junior squad in Stirling.'*

'Gibney was known as "Mr Swimming" in Ireland,' the article went on, *'but his former swimmers would paint a different picture of him; that of an insidious child molester.*

'*Each of the witnesses, obtained by the* Sunday Tribune, *has said they are willing to testify against Mr Gibney. For the present, however, we have decided to maintain their anonymity and apply fictitious names to their account of what happened to them. The accounts appear on pages two and three.*'

I was rattled. *There was more than this front page!* I read on, not daring to think of the horror of pages two and three. A reporter, it told us, had travelled to Scotland and called to the house where Gibney was staying. Conveniently, he was not in, but when the journalist outlined the allegations against Gibney, the teaching scheme co-ordinator of the swim club replied, '*This was all discussed at George's interview. If anything did happen, it was long ago, in the past.*' She continued, '*There is always another coach on the deck. This could not happen in our club.*'

I paused. *You fool!* I thought. Much of my abuse occurred with another coach on the deck and other parents around as well, including my own!

'*When told of the* Sunday Tribune *allegations against Gibney, she said that there was no reason for her club to dismiss the Irishman.*'

I felt defeated, whatever fight I had within me seeping out of the wounds of her words. She knew the allegations, yet chose not to believe us. This was exactly what I had feared. I re-read the page until I almost knew it off by heart, taking in more detail with every reading.

I stood, and walked around the bedroom a couple of times before going into the bathroom. When I looked in the mirror, a crimson-red face looked back. Cupping my hands under the cold tap I splashed my face a few times, the cool water taking some of the heat out of it. Looking once more in the mirror, the voice in my head coaxed me to have courage. I nodded. *I can do this.* Returning to my bed, I removed the book from Gibney's face and quickly turned to pages two and three. An almost life-size photo of Gibney's face stared back at me.

Coach: 'Take off your togs and wait'

The heading was in large print across both pages. I grabbed the book and once again hid Gibney's face, but there was nothing I could do to hide the headline. What poor child had remembered that quote? I began to shake from head to toe with a coldness that had nothing to do with the lack of heat in the bedroom and everything to do with remembering just how cruel Gibney had been.

Gary O'Toole's three-year fight to 'out' Gibney
Three years of forced sexual activity
Sportsman was 'brilliant but devious'
The priest said: 'Tell him to stop'
'Gibney had become very friendly with my parents'
'He told me to tell him I liked what he was doing'

I curled up on the bed and closed my eyes. Oh my God! This was a hundred times worse than I had ever imagined. I didn't want to read any more … but somewhere beneath those titles was my story.

I began to read, transfixed. Betty, Pauline, Linda, Cathy: fictitious names telling the stories we couldn't tell in person. I had to keep pausing, the details too graphic at times, as a storm of emotions jostled within me – nausea, rage, sadness, hurt, and more. As I read the testimonies of these strangers – laying bare cruelties and horrors of a most intensely private nature – I felt their childhood bewilderment, disgust and fear as keenly as I had my own. It was deeply shocking and sad to know that Gibney had been destroying young lives years before he'd ever come near me, and that there had been more after me.

Reeling from it all, I took some time before I plucked up the courage to look at my own piece. It was a quarter of a page in size beneath the fake name Johnny had given me. As I began to read it, I was transported once more to Blackrock garda station, hearing my quiet, faltering voice reading my statement. I remembered a guard patiently coaxing me to speak up, while another wrote down all that I said, word for word, and as I read, I remembered every word, every story, every detail.

Doors of rooms I'd hoped I would never again see inside, opened: his office, the Newpark school library, other parts of the school, his home when I stayed overnight after babysitting, his car, driving me to and from competitions, picking me up after school. Abroad or down the country, when he entered my hotel room. I remembered the furniture, the carpet tiles on the floor, his crushing weight and scratching beard. Gibney was back in the room. I could see him. I hated him, but that hate was secondary to the pain. Physical pain, bearing down and burning in my chest as I remembered the horror of the many days and nights endured by my young teenage self, and my absolute certainty that there was no way out. The intensity of that remembered feeling, of being imprisoned in plain sight, caught me unawares, reminding me of the loneliness and desperation I had felt during those years and the bleakness of the future I believed lay ahead.

I remember being fifteen years old, cycling at speed down the hill from my house to school, racing to outrun the memories of the morning's particularly distressing assault as they chased me. Taking the corner at the end of the hill, the heavens opened – a thunder plump, as my mum would call it. Within seconds I was soaked, rain from my sopping hair dripping down my face. Wiping the rain from my eyes, I cycled on, feeling cold and utterly wretched. I began to cry, the driving rain a perfect camouflage for my tears. I was not a crier as a rule, but on my bike that morning I couldn't stop. I felt hopeless, trapped, miserable. My life would never be normal. There would be no falling in love, no boyfriend, no marriage, no children. I would never be free, because he would never let me go.

22

A Call from the Guards

It's almost 7.30 p.m. and I am watching out the window of the sitting room, waiting for Gibney's car to pull up to take me to his house to babysit. I am fourteen years old. I feel neither dread nor fear as I wait – this is my life; I'm resigned to it. As he pulls up outside I shout my goodbyes to Mum and Dad, banging the front door behind me. Sitting into the car, Gibney smiles at me, and as we drive away begins to make small talk. My every nerve is instantly on high alert; his laugh is too forced, his voice too giddy, his driving too fast. I sit quietly in the passenger seat, not moving a muscle, staring straight ahead. Within the confines of the car, in the overpowering reek of his sickly-sweet aftershave, the sense of danger is at full pitch. As he races along, inwardly the shutting down process begins, as my body prepares itself for what lies ahead. I say nothing, just hope that, wherever he is taking me, whatever he has planned, it will be quick. Minutes from his house we take a turn in a different direction.

'We'll just go for a little spin,' he says, almost licking his lips as he looks at me.

I remain quiet, counselling myself to stay calm, stoic in my acceptance of what lies ahead. We drive for a few more minutes before he turns into the car park of a small *private hospital near his home. There are a few cars parked, but he drives past them to where it's dark and quiet. I continue to stare ahead as he turns off the engine. Within seconds my seatbelt is undone, and my seat flies back. Perhaps it's the speed of it all, or maybe it's because I am so on edge, but tonight my reflex action is to fight back. I push him away, hitting out, shouting for him to stop. But there is no stopping him. He is going to get what he wants, whatever the cost. And he does.*

When it is all over, he starts the car and we drive off. In the silence I sense him glancing in my direction now and again, but I stare ahead, my mind full of loathing for him. Close to his house, he begins to make small talk, but I ignore him. I imagine all the ways I might kill him.

Later, when he and his wife are gone out and the children are in bed, I try to watch television, but I can't get past what happened. The evening's assault replays over and over in my mind, as if I were outside myself, watching it on a CCTV screen: Gibney's car entering the hospital car park and driving towards the darkest corner. I flinch at the remembered click of the belts unlocking and the shock of my seat flying back. Gibney's face, inches from mine, his beard, his glasses, his breath. I blink, trying in vain to stop the scene playing out, as I sit alone, tearless, violated and defeated.

The sudden ring of the doorbell startles me. It's late and the children are asleep. Afraid that if it rings again it might wake them, I rush to get it, opening the door just enough to peep out. On the doorstep are two guards.

'Hello,' they say, 'do you live here?'

'No, I'm just babysitting. This is the Gibneys' house. George and his wife are gone out.'

They are just making inquiries, they tell

me. Taking out a notebook, one of them asks does Mr Gibney own a certain model and colour of car and, consulting his notebook, he calls out a registration number. I've no idea if it is the correct reg, but I do know it is the right colour and model of car. I tell him so.

'Okay,' he says. 'It's just that earlier this evening we got a report from St Gabriel's Hospital about a car parked in the car park and we were just following it up.'

I feel my face flush red. Had someone heard me shouting?

'Em, I don't know anything. Sorry.'

'What time did they go out?'

'I think about seven thirty?' I lie, as that was the time Gibney had collected me.

'Thank you,' says the guard, putting his notebook away. 'You might tell Mr Gibney we called and ask him to get in touch with us?'

I nod, closing the door, my hands shaking,

before I tip-toe upstairs to check the children. Thankfully, the late-night callers haven't disturbed them. Returning to the sitting room I'm unnerved, wondering what Gibney will say. What will he do, now that someone has witnessed his attack and called the guards? In dread, I watch the time tick by until they arrive home but inside part of me is singing. Surely, this will make him stop.

When he returns home, I tell him about the guards calling as soon as his wife is out of earshot. He doesn't blink an eye, just laughs and says he'll sort it out in the morning. I go to bed feeling as if a door that had opened briefly has been slammed shut. The following morning, as he drops me home, neither of us mentions the night before.

My hope that this garda visit would signal the end of things was short-lived. I never did find out what he told them, but the incident was never again mentioned, and the abuse continued unabated. Years later, I recounted this episode in my statement to the guards. They said they would see if there was a report on file, but I never heard if they followed it up or found any record of it.

The memory of that night is one of my more frequent flashbacks. It can strike me at any time or in any place. As it unfolds, I tend to stop the reel rolling as I close the door on the guards. Unlike some of my other flashbacks, which leave me frightened or upset, this one leaves me with a deep sense of sorrow as I recall that abused, sore, frightened child and the agony of her silence that night. I had been offered the chance to escape; two guards arriving at my door while I was alone in the house. I had only to speak up, to tell them what Gibney had done to me in the car park, to say to them I was frightened and that I wanted it to stop. Instead, the wounded teenager I was stood mute, afraid that if I spoke out, it would be me in trouble with the guards.

In my twisted thinking, Gibney was a married man with children, a pillar of society, a respected coach. And I was a bad person.

Despite knowing and understanding now why I didn't speak out, it is still difficult to quell the inner voice that says I could have stopped it, I should have stopped it. Yet even as I condemn myself, I remember my shame, guilt and unquestioning obedience to Gibney. What many fail to understand is that breaking the silence of abuse takes more than courage; it takes time, healing and the understanding that I was a child and he an adult. This is why sexual abuse is so often prosecuted as an historical crime.

Looking back, my decision to go to the guards was probably made too soon. I had no time to process my hurt, no time to ready myself to tell Eamonn, my family or Mum and no time to properly prepare myself for telling the world in the *Sunday Tribune*. Waking the day after it was published, I felt no relief, only guilt and shame. Fragile to the wounding words of the public, I waited to see what the fallout would be. It was catastrophic.

I knew nothing of the impact that Monday, as I hid away, ardently avoiding the many reports on radio and in newspapers, convinced that everyone I knew had read the *Tribune* and guessed who I was. I couldn't even face my friend Olive, declining her invitation to call to her house with the little ones that afternoon. However, she was not one to give up easily and by the evening I'd agreed, under duress, to go out for a drink with her after the children were in bed.

As I readied myself to meet her, I was filled with dread. Eamonn arrived home with the news that the papers were full of the story and asked did I want to see them. I hesitated.

'Gibney's photograph is in them,' he said.

I shook my head. 'Definitely not.'

Yet, not reading them didn't free me either, as imagining what they said was almost as bad or maybe even worse. I couldn't believe I had agreed to meet Olive and wondered how I could excuse myself. All I wanted to do was curl up in bed and forget about the world.

Thinking about my story, under my fictitious name, sickened me. The most intimate details of the abuse – my deepest, most private hurt – had been printed in black and white for all to read, to discuss, to scrutinise. What would people think? What judgement would they make of me?

As Olive's car pulled up, I knew there was no backing out. I gave Eamonn a quick goodbye kiss and he hugged me tight, an unspoken *You'll be okay*. I squeezed him back my silent *Thank you*. Unlike my usual quick dash out the door as I escaped for a night out, I walked slowly to Olive's car, willing myself to hold it together. Once inside, I closed the door and for the briefest of moments I thought I would be okay, that we would say a cheery hello, smile and drive off as we had done many times before. But as we shared a look and I saw the sympathy and hurt in her eyes, I crumbled. Olive reached across and we hugged one another in silence, a moment of intense friendship shared within the confines of the car, as the tears fell.

'Do you know how hard it was for me to read that about my friend?' she said, her voice breaking as we let each other go.

'Why did you read it?' I cried. 'I didn't want you to read it!'

'Well, I'm sorry, but I did. He's a bastard.'

'He sure is,' I said, and we both laughed out loud at her somewhat understated description of Gibney and the conviction behind it. The ice had been broken, the awkwardness of our first meeting over. I don't remember much of our conversation afterwards or of other first meetings I had with family or close friends, but I do know there was very limited discussion with anyone. It was just too hard. Indeed, it would be many more years before I was comfortable letting those outside my close circle of family and friends know that I was a survivor of Gibney's abuse, and twenty-five years before I would be comfortable linking my name in the media with Gibney.

23

Why Don't
They Believe Us?

In the days after the *Tribune* exposé, media interest
was intense, and in my fragile state it was very
difficult to deal with. On the Monday I avoided
tuning in altogether, but by Tuesday I was a little
braver. The headlines were full of the story.

Sports world stunned

It's a conspiracy

It was surreal to know I was making the news,
even if I was not identified. One of the survivors

bravely went public on Pat Kenny's radio show, while maintaining his anonymity. I cried as I listened to him, his story so raw, his hurt palpable. I was stunned by his courage and hugely grateful that he spoke out, for by doing so he gave credence to all our stories. However, overall I felt generally unsupported, especially after reading the quote from the Irish Amateur Swimming Association (IASA).

Swimming world 'upset by abuse claim'

'The IASA is terribly embarrassed and upset by the reports alleging long-term and persistent sex abuse by the coach George Gibney, the president said. A special committee has been set up, "to handle the present situation and to examine getting in a Stay Safe type programme".'

'Terribly embarrassed and upset'! I couldn't believe it. Not even 'upset and embarrassed'! The previous day, I learned, they had issued a statement declaring that, 'On legal advice we're not saying anything at this time.'

Now here they were finally commenting,

without a single word of regret that this had happened to children in the care of their organisation. I could feel the wheels of legal-speak begin to turn, and we were in danger of being thrown under the bus. This had been my fear all along, ever since the call telling me Gibney had got off; without a conviction we were always going to be 'alleged victims'.

The following day, Wednesday, the furore continued.

Minister seeks report on sex abuse allegations

I wanted to hide. We were now featuring in the Dáil! The minister for sport had asked for a report from the IASA, as Gary had revealed publicly that he had reported Gibney to the Leinster branch in 1992, around the same time as he sent me the letter, but instead of investigating the allegations they had gone to a solicitor. Following his legal advice, they had done nothing, and not long afterwards they had run a course for young swimmers with Gibney as coach.

Waking up and facing each day was becoming

more difficult, wondering what the headlines would say. Tired and emotional, Thursday proved to be particularly difficult.

Swimming coach in sex allegations safe in new job

I'd had no idea what might happen after we went public, but I had hoped it would mean that people would no longer trust Gibney with their children, that they might at least wonder if we were telling the truth. Reading that headline was upsetting as it looked like I'd been wrong. Had going to the guards and upsetting my family all been for nothing?

'"_There have been allegations but until they're proven in a court of law, then we have no comment on them whatsoever," a spokesperson for his Scottish swim club said … As far as they were concerned it was "good media fodder"._'

This was like a kick to my stomach. Eamonn pointed out that lots of people were hugely sympathetic, but it wasn't enough. Those who should believe us, didn't. Gibney's new club, Warrender, in Scotland, didn't. The parents of the children at risk didn't and the IASA and most within the world of swimming didn't. I felt utterly defeated.

Saturday's headline turned things in a new direction.

Parents want Gibney sacked

My heart soared. *'Irate parents have accused the club of playing Russian roulette with the safety of their children. Gibney, who has always protested his innocence, avoided television crews outside the club yesterday by hiding in a nearby supermarket before being smuggled into the coaching session.'*

After a long week, this was the happiest of news. Television crews were following him. He had to hide in a supermarket. They were demanding his sacking. My sisters rang, having read the article, and we laughed out loud, letting our imaginations go wild as we pictured the scenes of angry Scottish parents and the press forcing Gibney to hide. For the first time I looked forward to the nine o'clock news, delighting in thoughts of his discomfort. Monday's news was even better.

Club fires Gibney

Just one week after the *Tribune* article, we had got what we wanted. Gibney was no longer coaching. In fact, word was that he had 'fled'. No one knew where to, but he was gone. There was at least one child in Scotland who would have the future they deserved. News reports told of the sacking after 'more information' was received. I didn't know whether to laugh or cry. It was our first victory.

The next few weeks flew by. With Christmas approaching, I was busy shopping and decorating. Media interest in Gibney remained high. How had it happened? Who knew? Why had it taken the efforts of one parent, who contacted the Irish guards for information, to push the Warrender club to have him removed? Why not the committee? Where had he gone? There appeared to be two schools of thought: one full of horror and upset for the survivors and fury at the IASA, the other firmly of the opinion that he didn't face court because our allegations were malicious and untrue.

Much of that time is lost to me now, the days

running into weeks, the stories and headlines jumbled. However, there are clear memories which have lingered, the depth of the hurt they caused at the time never forgotten.

One was a letter, written by a former swimmer, which appeared in the *Tribune* on Christmas weekend, three weeks after our story was published. ***Gibney allegations*** was its heading. Reading it, I felt as though every word was addressed to me personally. The strength of his belief in Gibney, and therefore his disbelief in my story, was obvious. The *Sunday Tribune*, he wrote, had '*acted as prosecution, jury, judge and executioner. Mr Gibney has lost his house, his family, his job and essentially his country.*'

The letter went on: '*It is an extraordinary arrogance, if not a contempt of court, that you have sought to destroy this man in such an unbalanced way. If there is an opportunity to say that despite the allegations which stand against him, there is much that is good in George Gibney, I hope that you will permit me to express that view.*'

I sat for a while, winded, the words 'there is much that is good in George Gibney' delivering a killer punch. Eamonn came into the kitchen and I pushed the paper towards him, shaking my head. He began to read it and I studied his face, watching to see what his reaction might be to that final sentence. He took some time, perhaps reading it more than once, before he looked up, his thoughts written all over his face.

'Why would anyone write that?' I asked, hearing the break in my voice. 'Why would he think I'm telling lies? I've small children. Why would I lie?'

'I don't know, Trish,' was all Eamonn could say, not bothering with platitudes, knowing there were no words that would comfort me. In hindsight, I appreciate better the thinking of the writer and bear him no malice. He was a product of the time and spoke the thoughts of many within the swimming community. But that Christmas Eve, reading his words of defence for Gibney, I was crushed, the fight within me temporarily snuffed out. We had done all we could, I had done all I could, and it wasn't enough.

Christmas came and went, and as we rang in the New Year, I doubt there were many who said goodbye to 1994 as robustly as I did, full of hope that 1995 would be brighter. My New Year resolution was simple: to let Gibney go. There was nothing more I could do, and people's opinion was just that, their opinion. Those in my life, who I cared about, believed me. Unfortunately, however, like many of my previous New Year resolutions, by the end of January it was forgotten, its death accelerated by a newspaper report.

The IASA had held a meeting during which they debated whether they should revoke Gibney's life membership, an honour bestowed on those who have given great service to the sport of swimming in Ireland. The decision was taken that, for the present, he would remain a life member.

'There is a formal procedure for removing people from membership and natural justice demands that it should be followed.' [The speaker continued], 'The *association would have to get a written complaint asking for the removal of Mr Gibney and stating the reasons for the request.'*

I tried hard to 'let it go', but it was very difficult having to read words such as 'natural justice' and the association hiding behind procedural practices, almost laying the blame at our feet for not sending in our 'complaints' in writing, while never acknowledging the fact that children under their care were hurt. The following evening, I was still simmering when Eamonn came home with another newspaper.

Ex swim coach Gibney 'a broken man'

This was the quote of a man well known in Irish swimming, and to me personally. He said that Gibney had contacted him over Christmas and was *'clearly a broken man'*. He'd known him for over thirty years and *'never saw anything that would substantiate the allegations. I think it should all be laid to rest now, unless someone is willing to put in a formal complaint.'*

Perhaps it was because I knew this official, but

his words cut me as deep as if a member of my family had spoken them.

'Why not ring him?' said Eamonn.

I'd been so careful of my anonymity that it had never occurred to me to come out of hiding, until Eamonn suggested it. Immediately, I knew that that was what I wanted to do, what I had to do.

Scouring the telephone book, I pinpointed an address and number most likely to be his. Nervous but determined, I dialled it, and he answered. I cannot remember what we said, but the upshot of it was that he agreed to come to my house.

The day arrived, and as his car pulled up outside, Eamonn asked if I'd like him to stay for the meeting.

'No,' I said, 'I want to see him alone.'

This official was a big man, dwarfing me as we stood in my sitting room. I wasn't intimidated or fearful as we faced each other, as prior to the article I'd considered him to be a kind father. He took a seat on the couch opposite me, the atmosphere awkward and tense, as Eamonn introduced himself, offered tea and left us. I didn't mess around with pleasantries but came straight to the point, and as I began to talk, the words tumbled out. It was my first time speaking of the abuse to someone who was not a friend or member of my family, other than the guards. The first – and only – time I ever spoke to someone involved in swimming who backed Gibney.

It was all true, I told him. I was thirteen. There was abuse. Rape. It happened on trips he had been on. He had missed all the signs. I watched as this giant of a man shrank in front of me, the body language of his despair obvious. His shoulders sagged as he sat shaking his head, his eyes full of hurt. As he listened without interrupting, I was initially merciless, wanting him to know how much his words had hurt me, but as I saw the toll my own words were having on him, his quiet acceptance of them and his obvious regret, I backed off. By the time our conversation was over it was *me* who was feeling sorry for *him*. Like so many others, he had been manipulated and used by Gibney.

'I'm sorry,' he told me, and those simple words meant everything. Looking back, I will always be grateful that he had the courage to call to my house. It was certainly not something he had to do, as a phone conversation was all I had expected, but he did, and he listened, accepted my story and apologised, and I have never forgotten it. To date, he is the only person involved in Irish swimming at that time to ever offer me an apology for their actions or inactions.

24

Facing the Past

In 1998, my seven-year-old daughter Aoife asked a question I was not prepared for. It was four years after we'd heard Gibney would not face trial. I was slowly picking up the shattered pieces of my life, but the legacy of abuse was ever present. Although I was living in a different city to where most of my abuse had taken place, Cork was not without its own triggers.

On occasions I passed a certain city centre hotel,

with a child's hand in mine, or with Eamonn by my side on a night out. Each time, memories were unleashed, of being raped by Gibney, age fifteen, in a toilet there. In the hours after the rape, I had competed in a pool near the town, now our local pool. It was there that my friendship with Gary O'Toole had officially ended, that afternoon.

Mostly when I passed the hotel – walking on, never saying a word – I'd push aside those memories, but sometimes I'd let them linger, acknowledging the abused young girl within me and what she'd endured.

So when Aoife asked a simple, innocent question – one that in any other circumstance would have given me delight – it sent a wave of panic through me: 'Mum, can I join a swimming club?'

Having dropped the bomb, she wandered off, leaving me to 'think about it'. And I did. For weeks my heart and head debated at length as she continued to pester me. She was already able to swim, as I had taken her to a small pool some distance away for lessons, but allow her to join a club? With a coach and training sessions? No chance. Yet was this not just another challenge to be faced? Was I going to allow Gibney to dominate my own children's future?

A simple 'yes' was all Aoife heard, as my head eventually ruled my heart, but as she raced off to tell Eamonn, I instantly regretted my decision. A few weeks later, as I packed her bag for her first evening at the club, I was far from convinced. Driving into the pool's car park an hour later, I knew I wasn't ready for this, and my fear only intensified as I opened the door into the pool's reception area. A cocktail of chlorine and heat hit me, the remembered smell filling my lungs with a fear bordering on terror, transporting me back to a different pool, a different time, when to go for a swim meant passing his office, praying the door would not open. I looked about, reassuring myself that this was not that pool, that Gibney was nowhere near, but my panic continued to rise.

The busy reception area was packed with

parents and noisy, excited young swimmers, many already wearing their swim hats, waiting to register. I tried to centre myself in the present, but the past surrounded me and the desire to flee was overwhelming. I looked towards the exit wondering if I could make some sort of excuse and leave, but as I did a small hand slipped into mine – little Aoife, unnerved by the crowd, looking to me for reassurance. I squeezed it gently, as much to calm myself as my daughter. Taking a deep breath, I stepped into the crowd and waited our turn to give our names. With the dash of a pen it was done, Aoife was a member of Sundays Well Swimming Club (SWSC).

Walking down the corridor to the dressing room, I noted that even the tiles on the walls seemed familiar, the dressing rooms exactly as I remembered them. Having shown Aoife the way into the pool, I retraced my steps to reception, walked through to the viewing gallery and made my way to sit opposite the group Aoife was swimming in. For the briefest moment I paused, close to the spot where cross words, hurt and misunderstanding had robbed fifteen-year-old me of my friendship with Gary. Sadness washed over me as I remembered that young pair and all we lost that day.

Taking a seat midway down the pool, my thoughts bounced between the past and present, returning Aoife's waves and smiles one minute, while a minute later remembering that I was sitting only feet away from where Gibney had sat, warning with just a look that I'd better not tell anyone what he'd done. An hour later, as Aoife ran in the door of our home to tell Eamonn all her news, I felt no sense of achievement at my having the courage to go to the pool. Instead, my mind spun at the Pandora's box of memories that had been set free.

'How did you get on?' asked Eamonn.

'Great,' I lied.

For months, I struggled, sometimes even more than I had that first night, the mere thought of bringing Aoife to the pool making me anxious and afraid. However, she was enjoying her swimming, and gradually my anxiety began to lessen. Then something magical happened. As I watched my daughter fall ever more deeply in love with swimming, my own childhood memories began to rewind, to before Gibney and my early days of the sport. As they did, I was able to untangle my love of swimming from the horror of abuse, and one night, as I looked at the empty pool after Aoife's class finished, for the first time in fourteen years I felt the desire to dive in. The feeling continued to grow stronger with each pool visit, until finally one day I told Eamonn that I wanted to swim again. I wasn't sure if I was ready, but I knew I was ready to try.

I'm not sure what Eamonn thought when I made my big announcement. Perhaps he imagined I was healed, or maybe he feared for me. Whatever his thoughts, as I left for my first night with Sundays Well Masters, he said nothing, and neither did I, although at every roundabout and traffic light I was tempted to turn back. I could see my gear bag sitting on the passenger seat. Inside it was a towel, a pair of togs, swim hat and goggles. My stomach somersaulted as the smell of chlorine hit me, wafting up from the gear bag, despite the fact that the bag was shut, and the brand-new togs had never been in a pool. Why was I putting myself through this? Yet, as I wondered, my inner voice egged me on, not only assuring me I could do this but insisting I should.

In the dressing rooms I quickly pulled on my togs, fearing I might change my mind, and a few minutes later, my every nerve on edge, I walked onto the pool deck. The once familiar sound of the rhythmic splashes of the swimmers already in the pool calmed me, as a softly spoken Masters swim coach welcomed me to the club. Giving no indication of my previous swimming experience, I slunk off to a side lane, but as I pulled on my cap and goggles and stepped towards the edge of the pool, I felt excited and giddy at the prospect of getting in. I waited for a space in the lane to appear and dived in.

The cool water seeped through my skin and into my soul as I drifted at speed along the bottom of the pool. Exhilarated, I glided along, watching the tiles below me flash past as the pool became deeper. There was no past or future, only this moment. But with my lungs demanding air, I kicked hard to the surface, feeling more alive than I had felt in years. Length after length I swam, my lack of fitness obvious, but the greater the burn in my arms and legs, the louder my heart sang. Like reuniting with an old friend, I'd forgotten how big a place swimming held in my life and how much I'd missed feeling weightless, unburdened, free.

For forty minutes, I felt whole. As I clocked up the mileage, I thought a lot about the angry, confused teenager I had once been, remembering her thoughts as she swam up and down the pool for hours every day, all those years ago. For teenage me, the pool had been a sanctuary, the water my closest friend and confidante. In it I had unleashed my anger, cried my tears and dreamed my dreams. As a competitive swimmer I'd learned lessons in courage, strength, determination and resilience. Returning to the pool felt like both an ending and a beginning.

For eighteen years I remained a member of Sundays Well Swimming Club, diving back in as a swimmer, a teacher and a coach. It was a joy to not only teach hundreds of children and young adults to swim but to watch so many of them fall in love with a sport that I loved. Swimming had never hurt me, Gibney and an inept organisation had.

Having taken that leap back into the pool, I allowed myself a pat on the back and even wondered if perhaps it proved I was 'healed'. Unfortunately, it didn't take long for me to discover that it brought with it a whole host of fresh challenges.

First up was the challenge to compete again. Not long after my return to swimming there was a small local gala taking place in a nearby pool. Would I take part, my team asked. 'I might be away that Saturday,' I replied, thinking I would make sure I was. But as the entry deadline came closer, I wondered could I do it. Did I want to compete again? Unaware of my worries, my team-mates continued to pile on the pressure, and I eventually gave in, thinking, *It's now or never*. One month later, standing on the starting blocks ready for my first race, Gibney didn't enter my head, and I relished the prospect of competing once more. Later that evening, when I told Eamonn I'd enjoyed my day, I was not lying.

My next hurdle was as a coach, not a swimmer. I was to attend a competition as coach to a group of young swimmers, in a pool identical to the one in which I'd swum as a child. A sports complex with a similar office door at the end of the corridor, similar dressing rooms, similar showers, tiles and pool. I dreaded going and wondered if it was worth it. I was doing well, why risk going backwards? But surely by not going, Gibney was winning. So, early one Saturday morning, stopwatch in hand, I entered the all-too-familiar-looking complex.

That first day of the competition I avoided walking down the corridor, ensuring I didn't have to pass the office. After all, standing on the pool deck was trauma enough. However, by the second day I knew I would have to face it, and after lunch I took a deep breath and walked into the complex and down the corridor. Instead of batting away my thoughts, I let them roll; thirteen-year-old me, gear bag in hand, walking along, her footsteps too loud. He would hear them. Was his door open or closed? Relieved it was closed, I'd quicken my step, the dressing rooms in sight, only to hear the sickening sound of the door opening and a low whistle. As I allowed myself to remember, I was surprised to realise that instead of feeling frightened, upset or sad, all I felt was anger. The bastard! Later that afternoon, as I high-fived my young charges after their good swims or comforted them in their disappointments, my anger gave way to sadness, as I thought of the wonderful memories my swimmers were making for themselves and the memories I should have had.

One of my final challenges in swimming was to

compete in an all-Ireland competition alongside swimmers who had known me during the abuse. I'd been back swimming some time and had successfully avoided such galas, but once again I was being put under pressure by my team-mates. Would I go with them? The competition was in Tralee. We'd stay over. It would be great fun. I was torn. I did like the idea of going away with the team for a night, but the thought of coming face to face with my past, meeting those swimmers I'd not seen since I was a teenager, filled me with dread. Did they know I'd been one of those abused by Gibney? What would I say to them?

Once again, partly due to my team-mates' pressure and partly to ensure Gibney did not win, I agreed to compete, and late one Friday evening arrived at the pool with some of my oblivious SWSC friends. There was a big entry to the gala and the pool was buzzing. Almost immediately I spotted a few swimmers I recognised, despite not having seen them in almost twenty years. Competing against me was an ex-swimming friend of mine from Dublin. She'd swum with another club when we were teenagers and we'd been great rivals and friends. I was shy to speak to her, but she was as warm and friendly as ever and as we showered after our race we chatted easily, filling each other in on what was happening in our lives. I don't remember which one of us finally addressed the elephant in the room but when we did, I didn't hesitate to answer her.

'Yes, Gibney abused me.'

She wasn't surprised. In fact, her biggest surprise, she said, was to see me looking so happy. She told me that another swimmer competing that evening, who also knew me as a teenager, had seen me across the pool earlier and asked, 'Is that Patricia McCahill?' As they had both looked, wondering if it was me, the swimmer had laughed. 'No, it couldn't be her,' she said, 'she's smiling.'

Returning home the following day, I was glad to have jumped another hurdle but I couldn't shake the terrible sadness I felt as I remembered that swimmer's remark and the misunderstood girl she had spoken of who no one saw smile.

25

Everyone Has a
Gay Byrne Story

Approximately six years after I'd first told Mum about Gibney's abuse, our relationship reached an all-time low. Before my telling her, we would have phoned each other once a day or more and enjoyed lengthy chats about everything and nothing. Now we were lucky if we spoke weekly, of nonsense neither of us cared about, while the important things were left unsaid. Gibney was back in the news as Derry O'Rourke had been jailed for twelve years for sexual abuse (and he received a further ten years in another trial). Initially, he had used the same defence Gibney had, that the time delay was too great for him to provide an adequate defence, but the courts had now ruled that defence was no longer admissible, so prior to his trial he pleaded guilty. The almost daily reports in the papers and on radio and television were taking their toll on Mum and me.

I was consumed by my feelings of anger and injustice and was oblivious to any pain or sadness Mum might be feeling. Gibney had effectively driven a large wedge between us, the cracks in our relationship filled with hurt and misunderstanding, our festering silence slowly poisoning the close bond we had once shared. My visits home had become irregular and Mum's visits to me almost non-existent. Following the birth of my third child Naoise, I felt Mum's absence more than ever, but I couldn't see any way back.

Sweeping the kitchen floor one morning, I sighed, hissing like a deflating balloon at my dissatisfaction with my lot in life. Home twelve hours a day, with my three children aged eight, five and two, along with the two children I minded, I despaired. Was this all life had to offer? The radio was blaring, Gay Byrne's voice filling the silence of the kitchen, he or Gerry Ryan my usual morning companions. I was only half listening when I noted a change in Gay's voice, a sure sign something important or different was on its way. I stopped sweeping, straining to hear the faltering, quiet voice of the elderly gentleman Gay was talking to. 'Take your time,' Gay gently encouraged, while I held my breath, willing him on.

He'd barely begun to speak when I felt a tightening in my chest as I heard him struggle to find the words he'd never spoken before. He didn't need to tell me he had a secret. I could feel it. I recognised his hurt. I knew his agony. Now, in his seventies, the small boy within him was speaking out for the first time, while the grown man he'd become tried to explain the toll keeping that secret had taken on his life.

Time stood still. I was no longer a mother with an ear alert to possible happenings within the playroom, I was deaf to everything but this man's story, and as it tumbled out, it was my own voice I heard. This quietly spoken stranger was living my life, hurting with my hurt and crying my tears. As he spoke, suddenly I too wanted to be heard. I wanted my hurt and pain to be acknowledged, my everyday struggles understood.

Reaching for the phone, I called Mum.

'Hello?'

'Are you listening to Gay Byrne, Mum?' I blurted out.

There was a long pause. 'Yes,' she replied, her voice barely above a whisper.

'That's me, Mum,' I said, my voice breaking. 'You're listening to my story ... that's how I feel every day.'

'I know,' she replied, her voice soft and laden with tears. 'I'm listening.'

I hung up before the floodgates holding back my own tears burst open, but her words, spoken in her gentle Donegal accent, echoed in my head: *I'm listening*. Behind the sadness in her voice I picked up something I'd wanted to hear since that awful day when I had stood in the kitchen and first told her about Gibney: *I'm sorry you were hurt*.

I'm listening. As her words sunk in, a thaw began in the ice around my heart, rage and hurt seeping out, while the wounded child within me wanted nothing more than to race into the kitchen of my childhood home to be hugged and held by my mum.

The gentleman continued to tell his story. As I listened, it was not the sound of him softly crying or the harrowing account of his abuse I found painful, but the picture he painted of a small boy all alone with no one to hear his cries. How that picture resonated with me. When the interview ended I was devastated for him and, remembering my own experience, wondered if having told his secret, was he feeling even more broken than before.

Two small piles of dust gathered by my earlier sweeping reminded me of my forgotten task, but as I brushed them up my thoughts wandered back to my phone call to Mum.

From my earliest days Mum had been a constant in my life, the cornerstone of our family. Our home was filled with security, love and laughter, warmth and the smell of baking, Mum its epicentre. Although my mind did its best to erase much about my teenage years, I'd never given up those many happy memories of my childhood and Mum. Yet, as I picked up the phone that morning, they were far in the distance, overshadowed by the vivid recollection of my telling her about Gibney, and her reaction.

My melancholic meanderings were interrupted by the noisy arrival of the five little ones into the kitchen from the playroom, with demands for food. Oblivious to my mood, they clambered upon chairs, shouting over each other while I poured drinks and supplied biscuits, Naoise banging her cup, impatiently screeching 'more,

more'. *They will never remember this moment*, I thought, as I refilled their cups. How many such moments had I forgotten with my own mum? I looked at my eldest daughter, her eight-year-old eyes shining as she enjoyed the lively exchange at the table, and my heart skipped a beat: what would I do if she came to me as a young mother, with a secret such as mine?

As the day wore on, the red mists of anger, which I'd fuelled for so long, were beginning to dissipate. I thought a lot about the day I'd told Mum about Gibney, but instead of remembering it from the point of view of a daughter telling her mother, I viewed it from the perspective of one mother to another. What must it have felt like for Mum to be hit with that reality, without the solace and wisdom of a partner by her side? To have had no one to talk to, or cry with? No one to help her make sense of it all. As I began to see the events from her standpoint, a single thought flashed into my mind: was the gulf between us more of my making than Mum's? Was I the one pushing her away, while she clung on to whatever I would give her: a short phone call once a week, a brief visit every few months?

Shocked by the idea, I did all I could to dismiss the thought, but going to bed that night it was all I could think of. Was it true? Was it me who perpetuated the rift between us? As I lay there rethinking the past few years, arguing with myself the rights and wrongs of it all, I heard a voice speak as clearly as if it were someone beside me, *'You have a choice: do you want a relationship with your Mum in your future or not?'* Just the possibility of being close to Mum again filled me with a joy I'd not thought possible before the phone call that morning. *I had a choice.*

I woke the following day not feeling as forgiving as the night before. I had every right to be upset at Mum. I was the victim, the child. However, as my thoughts raged, I heard that voice once again whisper, *'You have a choice.'* I looked at the kitchen floor and imagined a single white line down the middle of it. On one side stood my anger and hurt, while on the other side stood Mum. There was nothing between the two, only that line. I could stand on one side with my anger and hurt or step over the line and be with Mum. If I did that, I would have to permanently leave behind my anger and hurt. I wasn't sure if I could do that or if I wanted to.

The morning wore on. I prepared breakfasts and busied myself with the little ones, but every now and then I paused to look at the imaginary line. *Was it so simple?* As I argued for and against, Gay Byrne's theme tune filled the kitchen. He began with his usual good morning, before telling us of the huge reaction the show had had to the gentleman from the day before. I recalled the elderly man telling his secret and Mum's voice, saying, *'I'm listening.'* Tears welled up inside me, spilling over. I wanted Mum. I wanted to call her and hear her tell me once again that she was listening.

Walking to my imaginary line, I stood on one side and looked across at the other. Could

I let my anger and hurt go? Yes, or no? I didn't pause, my mind made up. Lifting my leg in an exaggerated step, I crossed the line and stood on the other side of the kitchen, looking back at my imagined anger and hurt. The sense of relief was immediate. With Gay's voice chattering from the radio, I picked up the phone and made a call, and with a brightness I'd not felt in a long while I said, 'Hi, Mum.'

We never looked back. Leaving my anger and hurt behind was easier than I had imagined, and over time the relationship with Mum, which I'd thought was damaged beyond repair, healed and grew stronger than ever. Today, over twenty years later, Mum is gone and the choice I made that day takes on a new significance. I miss her desperately. I miss our chats, our texts, our laughter, our hugs. Yet I am beyond grateful that I do miss her. That the horror and hurt Gibney brought into our lives was not enough to destroy us, and the love we shared deep enough to see us through the darkness. Sometimes, when I think of that day, I remember the voice cutting through my anger and pain whispering, '*You have a choice*', and as I do I wonder, did I make that decision alone or could it be that Dad was not too far away, guiding me along and helping me through?

26

Leap of Faith

In the summer of 1987, when Dad was very unwell with motor neurone disease, he told us of his plan to write about living with MND, in an account that would be published in the newsletter of the support organisation for the condition in Ireland.

Dad was a beautiful writer and, with difficulty, could still use his typewriter. Daily, for weeks, he laboured on the old-fashioned contraption, his finger shaking as it hovered above often stubborn keys. Unlike the easy keyboards of today, each letter had to be struck with force to ensure it hit the ink band hard enough to make a mark. Sometimes I'd watch as he'd suddenly lower his finger, only to discover he'd hit the wrong key, like the claw in an amusement arcade game hovering over a cuddly toy before dropping and missing the prize. I avoided going near him, not because he'd ask for help, but because he wouldn't. Soon after the article was completed Dad lost the use of his hands. There would be no more writing.

Months later, the MND newsletter arrived with Dad's piece in it. We cheered and clapped him on the back, before we individually scurried off to our rooms with the newsletter tucked under our arms, choosing to wallow alone as Dad's words spoke to each of us. There were many who had looked at disabled Dad and thought the disease had made him become less, but reading his words it was plain to see he had become more.

'In the face of such darkness let me offer some

encouragement to fellow sufferers: be thankful that if
anyone in your family has to suffer, you are the one
and not them.'

As I lapped up every word he had written, I
cried reading his innermost thoughts and raged at
his acceptance of his lot, overwhelmed by his love
for us despite our failings.

'Remember it's far worse for those who have to
deal with you on a day-to-day basis. Their problem
is more long-term than your own. Their cross is
heavier than yours and it takes constant patience
and understanding on their part to cope with your
increasing invalidity.'

Each word in the article had a new value, as in
the weeks since composing it, Dad had not only
lost his ability to write, he had also been silenced,
the disease taking his voice, and just a few months
after the article appeared in the newsletter it
finally took him from our lives.

The days immediately after his death are a
blur, the pain of grief so strong I understood
how it was possible to die from a broken heart.

No tablets touched it. No words eased it. No hug took it away. Days became weeks and months. We went from a family of timetables, schedules and worry, to a freedom we couldn't remember, and yet despised. As Mum mourned the loss of her best friend, her children scattered, staying longer at college or out with friends, fleeing a house which, without Dad, no longer felt like home. Only Eileen remained, there to hold Mum's hand and help her through.

Some days hurt more than others: Sunday dinners at a table with an empty chair; my final nursing exam six weeks after losing him; and graduating without Dad there to tell me he was proud. Christmas came before we were ready, and with the New Year approaching, I wondered why time wasn't healing. Despite my lack of faith, I raged at the God my mother worshipped. Easter came and went, Dad's favourite time of the year, and then it was summer, bringing with it July 23rd, my parents' wedding anniversary, the first in thirty-two years Mum would spend alone.

I have little memory of the events of that day, for it is the following day which I remember. Opening the front door for Mum as she returned from mass and her daily visit to the graveyard, her morning's struggle was clear to see in her red eyes. We boiled the kettle for the obligatory cup of tea, our go-to comforter in times of trouble, and handed her the newspapers.

And it is there that we saw it, Dad's article, mid-way through the *Sunday World* newspaper, in Fr Brian D'Arcy's column. None of us knew it was to be printed, nor have we any idea how Fr Brian D'Arcy came to read it, but what did that matter? Dad was here, in our kitchen, at the table, beside Mum, sharing one last cup of tea on their anniversary weekend.

None of us would ever have thought that as Dad had laboured over each letter the year before, he was writing to us in the future, leaving Mum the best anniversary present he could give her. As we read the piece, over and over, his Donegal lilt and gentle voice filled the room one last time.

'Remember, to be taken suddenly may be a blessing, but it will leave forever a scar because no one had the chance to say goodbye.

'Life takes on a different set of values when you are faced with a difficulty you cannot overcome. Life is like a game, and regardless of your disappointment and often despair of your lot you must continue to play your part. Keep winding the clock that keeps you ticking, keep the fire within you burning and remember, "the darkness of the whole world is not enough to put out the light of even one small candle".'

Was it a coincidence or some sort of miracle? Who knows, but it is nice to imagine it was all part of the magic that was Dad, reminding us to live every day, be happy and never lose hope. Just as I like to believe that during the many dark days in my life, the light from that one small candle has continued to shine, guiding me through.

As the years have passed, the darkness I once lived in has receded, and for the most part I live in a brighter, happier world. However, there are days when the memories of the past emerge from the shadows, bringing with them nightmares by night and challenges by day. The long arm of abuse continues to reach into the lives of its survivors well after the violation has stopped, and this was brought home to me some thirty years after my last encounter with Gibney, around 2013.

Dropping my then eleven-year-old child, Caoimhe – our youngest – to school, she reminded me she had her music lesson that afternoon.

'Sorry, darling, we've to cancel,' I said. 'I've to collect Naoise in town.'

'Ah Mum! Why can't I go myself and you pick me up after?' There it was, the first punch thrown in today's battle. *Why indeed could she not go by herself?*

'No, I'm cancelling. It's easier, in case Naoise's bus is late,' I lied, and my easy-going, youngest child accepted my tale.

Leaning towards me, she kissed my cheek before skipping away, schoolbag and ponytail swinging as she turned in the school gate. Driving the short journey home, I continued to hear her simple question, why could she not go by herself? *Trust your instinct*, I thought. *One missed lesson wouldn't kill her.* However, my mind couldn't let it rest, and the nuns of my schooldays would have been proud as I continued to 'examine my conscience'.

Truthfully? Why not let her go?

I thought of the warm, kindly, middle-aged music teacher who greeted us each week. He thought I sat in for every lesson because I lived so far away. My daughter thought I stayed because I had a keen interest in her progress. Neither knew the truth. That in twenty years I'd never left any of my children alone in a room with a man, except their father, and even that had occasionally been a struggle. My head was pounding as I arrived home. Pouring myself a cup of tea, the arguments continued.

Who are you really protecting?
You are lying to yourself.
Do you not trust the teacher?

Although I knew my fear was irrational, I

struggled to keep up with the inner interrogation. Sitting at the kitchen table, I placed my face in my hands as a scene played out before me. I imagined myself at a football pitch, standing on the sideline with two teams lined up in front of me. One team was standing in the sun, calling me over, cheering me on:

'You can do this.'

'You're ready.'

'Are you going to let Gibney impact your children's lives too?'

The other team stood in the shade of the stand. They were quieter, heads down, kicking imaginary stones along the ground, muttering,

'Remember when you were that age?'

'Trust no one.'

'Do you really want to take the risk?'

I pictured the softly spoken teacher. Using the sixth sense I'd developed in relation to men, I was clear that this man was definitely in the 'I trust' bracket. *But could I ever really trust anyone?* I sighed as a part of me railed against my fears. This had gone on too long. How long was I going to let Gibney affect my life? I had to do this and today was the day.

The boardroom of my mind quietened as I announced my decision, and any further inner discussion on the matter was quickly shot down. Witnessing Caoimhe's delight later that afternoon when I told her I'd changed my mind, she could attend alone, only fuelled my resolve. However, less than five minutes later I wasn't so sure, as she jumped into the car, full of enthusiasm. My stomach turned head over heels, churning the contents of my lunch in true washing machine style. I glanced across at her smiling face as she chattered beside me, lit up by the story she was sharing. Imagine, I too was once an innocent child. *What was I thinking? Was this a gamble worth taking?*

I barely took notice of the road as I drove the short journey to her lesson, desperately trying to picture the kindly gentleman with the warm smile who would be waiting for her, not the goatee-bearded brute of my nightmares. My throat was parched, my tongue glued to the top of my mouth as we pulled up alongside his house, my heart beating so fast and loud I struggled to ignore it as we walked in the driveway. The teacher opened the door before we knocked, his smiling face full of welcome. Without hesitation, Caoimhe stepped into the hall, turning briefly towards me. 'Bye, Mum,' she said, and before I'd the chance to reply she shut the door.

Standing there, I stared at the closed door, struggling to catch my breath. It was as if a truck had come out of nowhere and rolled on top of me, crushing me as the girl of my childhood frantically banged on the ribbed walls of my chest, her high-pitched scream beseeching,

'GET HER OUT!'

'THEY'RE ALONE.'

'DON'T LEAVE.'

Nausea rose in my throat as I turned with legs of lead and walked away. Sitting into my car, I opened the windows and gulped fresh air like a drowning woman. I could clearly see through the large front-room window into the music room. Caoimhe and the teacher were sitting opposite each other, laughing as they shared a joke.

I gripped the steering wheel, my knuckles turning white. Hidden thoughts had begun to seep out of a room in some dark recess of my mind, a room I'd taken great care to lock for many years. Inside I glimpsed a smiling, tomboyish young girl in love with life. A girl I remember well. For a moment we looked at one another, before the door banged shut. It was the same colour as the music teacher's door and behind it I could hear her distant cries. I turned on the radio, put the car in gear and drove away, but as I stopped at traffic lights, she flashed in front of me once more. Unable to look away, I watched her slowly emerge from behind a different door, cautiously checking the corridor before coming out, her swim gear bag almost as big as herself. The lost, lonely, fragile child who hides in my every day.

Naoise was waiting for me as I arrived into

town. Sitting into the car, she didn't draw breath as she gave a blow by blow account of her day, never noticing my anxiety or the fact I kept looking at the clock. Bang on time we pulled up outside the teacher's house and Caoimhe ran out, beaming. I studied her in the rear-view mirror, searching for any hint of my mistake. I saw none.

The rest of the day ticked by in a haze, much of it spent swatting and ducking memories I'd no desire to recall, as I made dinner and corrected homework. Later that night, I went into Caoimhe's room to say goodnight. Sitting on her bed, I stroked her hair as she put away her book. Standing to leave, I brushed her cheek, rosy from the heat beneath her duvet, and bent to kiss her forehead. Inexplicable tears pricked my eyes as she reached up and squeezed me tight.

'Night, Mom.'

'Goodnight, sweetheart,' I said, turning off her light and closing the door.

Halfway down the stairs I paused to compose myself. In the distance, through the sitting-room double-door windows, I could see my three older children and Eamonn watching television. I stood for a moment, not yet ready to join them, but Aoife spotted me.

'Mum, you're missing this, it's brilliant.'

I slapped on a smile and stepped into the room. Barely taking his eyes off the screen, Eamonn reached for my hand as I eased myself between him and my daughter, blending into the scene. Sitting quietly, I stared at the television, but it was a different scene I was watching.

I was back at the football field of my morning's imagining, crossing the pitch towards the team in the sunshine, deafening applause from the imagined crowd ringing in my ears. Squeezing Eamonn's hand, a secret smile rippled through me. Today's battle had been tougher than most. There were no witnesses to my victory, no trophies to show my oblivious family. But today I had won this battle, which meant Gibney had lost.

27

Surprised by Joy

There is no rule book for surviving abuse, just as there are no guarantees of survival. While one person prevails, another is less lucky, and I don't believe the reasons why are simple ones. For me, there was always a conscious choice early on that my life would not be defined by abuse. It is a choice I make every day, and many days it is not the easiest choice available to me.

But there is something else too. I have within

me a tremendous drive to be happy, to laugh, have fun and enjoy every day of the precious life I've been given. It comes from never forgetting what it was like to live without knowing happiness, and from remembering the moment it returned to my life. It has marked my journey of survival, and for this I am eternally grateful. The first time I experienced this sensation of unexpected joy was in 1996.

It was two years after our case against Gibney had been dismissed, casting its long shadow into the heart of my daily life. A mother of two who minded two more, the daily routine was busy and chaotic. On this particular day I was relishing a short break from the kids, as Tiarnán and Jennifer, the baby I minded, were having their nap and Aoife and Jessica – Jennifer's sister – were on a playdate. I made myself a cup of tea and turned on the television, but after all of twenty minutes, Tiarnán decided he'd had enough napping.

'Hiya, hiya, hiya,' I heard him shouting.

My heart sank and I raced upstairs before he woke Jennifer. Entering his room, I saw he was standing at the foot of the cot, arms out, beaming in delight at my appearance. Ignoring his happy face, I rushed to get him downstairs as quickly and quietly as I could, shushing him along the way. I was halfway down the stairs when it happened. His two hands reached to my face and pulled my mouth into a smile. I paused mid-step to take his hands away and as I did, he exploded into the heartiest of giggles. It was so unexpected and infectious I burst out laughing. The depth of my laugh took me by surprise and as I continued down the stairs, I felt light-headed. Sitting Tiarnán on my lap on the sitting-room couch, I wondered had I jumped up too quickly when I'd heard him shouting. Tiarnán continued to smile and jump on my lap and as he did, I felt it again, that strange feeling, almost euphoric. This was not my usual everyday happy but something stronger, a happiness from somewhere deep within me. I tried to remember the last time I had experienced such a feeling, but I couldn't. I wondered if it was fleeting or if I would feel it again.

Thankfully, I did, many more times. That day something within me was unlocked, releasing true happiness back into my life, and I was determined to never again lose it.

Today, I continue to search for the happy in every day and when it comes, no matter how large or small the dose of it, I love nothing more than to laugh out loud. Gibney took a lot from my life but, as each smile or laugh reminds me, he didn't take everything. Back in 1996 there was still much healing to be done, but that afternoon I took one large step in the right direction.

Sometimes I still ask myself, 'Am I healed?' The answer is yes and no. Yes ... because today I can honestly say I live a happy and contented life. I've been lucky enough to meet someone who was never interested in healing me but patient enough to allow me find ways to heal myself and we have reared four children who make life crazy, fun and a joy to live. No ... because I am scarred, deeply.

Yet I no longer try to hide those scars. They show my strengths, not my weaknesses. They make me who I am.

In September 2020 the podcast 'Where Is George Gibney?' was finally released by BBC Sounds. The producer Mark Horgan had kindly allowed me to listen in advance to the episodes I featured in and such was his understanding of how difficult that might be, he advised me not only of the minutes I featured in, but also those in which I would hear Gibney's voice. Having received the advance recording, I didn't rush to listen, afraid of what I might hear and wondering if my belief that I would be okay after hearing it was just wishful thinking. That evening I told no one and took myself off for a walk, earphones in situ, curious and fearful to hear what parts of our conversation Mark had chosen to feature.

It was a glorious evening and as I walked, I quickly skipped through the podcast to my interview. Listening, I tried to imagine what Eamonn might think hearing it. Or my children. Did I say too much? Was it too graphic? Did it give hope? However, having heard my own interview a couple of times I relaxed, feeling relieved that Mark had stayed true to his word and not sensationalised my story.

Next, I plucked up the courage to listen to Ber Carley's story. Ber was the other survivor who spoke in the same episode. Her abuse had taken place a few years before mine. We'd not met as swimmers but had got to know each other during the podcast's production, each of us sharing a similar love of life and story of survival. Even though we both suffered abuse by Gibney, I found listening to her story deeply upsetting. She was just nine years old, and hearing her reminded me of the depths of Gibney's depravity and how isolated and alone we had once been. She also asked a question I've asked myself many times over the years, although she asked it more eloquently than I ever have:

'I often wonder what was I going to be like? The day he touched me did he squeeze and kill whatever I was going to be?'

Having listened to her, there was now only

one part of the episode I had yet to hear, the part featuring old footage of Gibney. I'd purposely chosen to go for a walk while listening, not wishing to contaminate any part of my home with memories of his voice. Just two seconds in I struggled, the short, clipped way he spoke and the tone of his voice triggering a sudden rush of intense panic and fear. I turned the link off and walked on, reassuring myself it was only a recording and that he no longer had power over me. It took a few minutes but, determined and a little more prepared, I tuned back in and managed to listen to the end, his voice, flashbacks, memories and feelings consuming me. I doubled back, extending my walk, not ready to go home yet.

As I began to regain control, I was relieved that the months of wondering and fearing the podcast were over. It was an excellent listen, but immediately it presented me with a new worry: what if it were a big success? I smiled at the speed at which I went from one worry to the next but a part of me was pleased that Mark's two years of effort had paid off and surely, having survived the media circus years ago, I'd get through this one.

Weeks later it was released to the world and the many messages of support poured in. What a contrast to almost thirty years ago, when we'd spoken out and so many had chosen not to believe us. Having already heard and lived it, the release day itself was not too difficult. However, it was not the same for my friends and family. They found it difficult to listen to and the common feedback was that they were 'not prepared'. As Eamonn said, 'I knew it had happened to you, I just didn't really appreciate what "it" was.' I found it difficult to know I was upsetting them, but their support, love and care for me was wonderful to receive. Indeed, even hearing my own voice recount some of my story left its mark on me.

'It was horrific,' I heard myself say during the interview. 'How did I live? How did I go to school? How did I go to sleep at night?'

Today, it is still hard to understand how I lived

that dual life as a teenager, but somehow I found a way. One day, during one of our many chats, Mark asked if I had any poetry which I liked to read or reflect on. I told him that when it came to my abuse, it was not poetry but rather a certain song which spoke to me. A song Michael had sent to me, written by Stephanie Bentley and Rob Crosby and sung by Martina McBride, called 'Concrete Angel'. In one verse, a few simple lines remind me of that young girl and the isolation and loneliness that were part of her every day.

'The teacher wonders but she doesn't ask
It's hard to see the pain behind the mask
Bearing the burden of a secret storm
Sometimes she wishes she was never born.

However, it is the chorus which speaks to me most, for it reminds me that even in the darkness I continued to dream and it was those dreams that gave me wings to fly from Gibney's abuse and dominance, home, to where I knew I was loved.

Through the wind and the rain

She stands hard as a stone
In a world that she can't rise above
But her dreams give her wings
And she flies to a place where she's loved
Concrete angel

Despite many dark days, 108 was that place, a place where I'd always felt loved.

Epilogue

Mum's Legacy

In March 2019, during Mum's last days, I was back home in 108. Sitting in the kitchen, I watched, pained, as her ailing body and mind struggled to fight sleep. She was sitting in her chair, her hand occasionally twitching, her head fallen forward, momentarily lifting before it dropped again as she drifted in and out of consciousness. I could feel the sands of time shifting, and I knew Mum's life was ebbing away, our remaining time together short. She'd been battling sleep for almost an hour, yet she refused to go to bed. Finally, after a large jolt she opened her eyes and looked around.

'I think I'll have to go to bed, Trish,' she said wearily. 'I'm very tired.'

Relief and sadness flooded through me, hearing the defeat in her voice, knowing the surrender was hard-granted.

'Will I get the wheelchair?' I suggested.

'No!' she said, loud and clear.

I despaired. How was she going to walk to her bedroom? I said nothing but placed her walking frame in front of her and helped her stand. *She must only weigh about six stone,* I thought, as I pulled her up.

'Too much sitting,' she said, as she tried to straighten up.

Her bedroom was no more than ten metres away, but it might as well have been a mile. I stood beside her as she attempted to take her first step, her right leg shaking with intent but steadfastly stuck to the floor. She continued her efforts to lift it as I willed her on, until finally it obeyed and she began to move. One tiny step, two, three. Stop. With each step she stooped lower, unable to support her weight, until her face was almost on top of her walker. We paused a moment, and as she straightened herself up again, her arms trembled from the effort. Once again, her legs refused to co-operate, but after another few failed attempts she finally took off, one baby step after another, trying to gain as much ground as possible before the inevitable next break.

'Pace yourself, Mum,' I said, as we reached the kitchen door, a quarter of the journey completed.

No sooner had I spoken than both her legs shook violently, and she began to crumble. I quickly grabbed a kitchen chair and she fell back into it. I exhaled, unaware I'd been holding my breath.

'Mum,' I said gently, kneeling before her, 'will we not get the wheelchair? You're very tired.'

'No,' she said, quieter than before.

'Why not, Mum?' I persisted. 'You can walk again later.'

'Patricia,' she said, lifting her head to look at me directly, 'if I get into that chair, I will never get out of it. I need to keep pushing myself.' And with that, the rest was over and we were on the move once more.

As she walked slowly on, I followed behind, watching her shuffling, stopping and starting, stubbornly bypassing the kitchen chair, placed just a few steps in front of her, determined to make it without sitting down again. Since I was a child I'd been told, 'You're so like your mother.' Occasionally I'd see a physical resemblance but overall I was of the strong opinion that I was nothing like Mum. *I sure hope I'm never as stubborn as her*, I thought, as the minutes ticked by. However, as I watched her painfully slow progress on the long trek to her bedroom, I began to appreciate more the excruciating effort she was making, and as I did, a surge of pride swept through me. Inwardly I began to cheer her on with every step she managed to take. It was an extraordinary feat. This tiny-framed, white-haired octogenarian was showing a strength and determination beyond anything I had ever seen in forty years of swimming and coaching. And as I swelled with pride at her spirit it suddenly hit me: *I was her!* How had I never seen it before? Mum's spirit, courage and strength was a part of me, a big part of what had seen me through, just as my grandmother's steely determination was a large part of Mum.

As we walked the final steps to her bed, I took in her frail body, her stoop, her shuffle, her determination, her strength, and I smiled as I looked into my possible future, thinking, *I hope, one day, I'll be every bit as stubborn as she is.*

Having finally made it to her bed, Mum almost fell into it, totally exhausted. I placed a gentle kiss on her forehead and quietly left the room. I was not to know that I had accompanied her on her final walk in life on her own two feet.

Since her passing I often imagine I hear her,

quietly advising me, laughing loudly or tut-tutting. Grief is a long process and losing both parents is life-changing, but I know that a large part of them lives on in me. And not only Mum and Dad but my grandparents and the generations before them, whose DNA courses through my body with every beat of my heart, who continue to live through me and whose voices will never be silenced.

George Gibney now lives in Florida, in the United States. He has never been tried for any crimes, but thanks to the Murphy Report, Gary O'Toole, Chalkie White, Johnny Watterson, Mark Horgan, Ciarán Cassidy and many more within the media, as well as some politicians, it is widely accepted worldwide that the crimes we alleged were committed, that the survivors told the truth. I have no yearning for Gibney to be returned for trial and am content to know that in my lifetime I will never again meet him.

Throughout my life I have fought many battles – some I have won, some I have lost. In my battle against Gibney there are many who believe I did not get the justice I deserve, but is there not justice in being able to say, I have lived a life, believed, happy and loved?

What more could I wish for?

Acknowledgements

I would like to thank and acknowledge the many who have been a part of the pages of this book, in both its creation and in the story it tells.

My agent, Faith O'Grady of the Lisa Richards Agency, you believed in this book before I did and found it a home at Hachette Books Ireland. Ciara Considine, editor extraordinaire, you saw beyond the chaos of my early draft and alongside talented editors Tess Tattersall and Aonghus Meaney have helped sculpt my words into the book it has become. Thank you also to Elaine Egan and all the team at Hachette Books Ireland for their ongoing support.

Cork Libraries. In your wisdom you appointed

Danny Denton and Denyse Woods as writers in residence. Danny, you were the first person I showed my stories to and your advice and encouragement were instrumental in my writing this book. Denyse Woods, your advice to look for an agent and your support of my writing were much appreciated.

My online writing community in Imagine, Write, Inspire, who are always just one click away, and all those bloggers and readers who have read my stories and ramblings on my blog, 'My Thoughts On a Page', over the years, especially Duncan, Colleen and Beth. The VIPB group, who have been there for me, quite literally, day and night. Nicola Cassidy, whose advice got me over a major writing bloc, and authors Andrea Mara and Casey King, who have been so encouraging and helpful.

To those in the 'real' world of writing, The Carrigaline Writers group, I look forward to showing you my words in print. Michelle and Nicola, for your advice and early reading of some of my stories. Tim Vaughan, who gave me my first ever writing gig in *The Examiner* and Irene Feighan, my editor there, for your patience and encouragement. Also, successful writers Carmel Harrington, Catherine Ryan Howard and Hazel Gaynor, whose words of advice at a weekend with *The Inspiration Project*, pushed me to write my first draft. Carmel, your ongoing support and belief in my writing has played an enormous part in my life.

Chalkie White, your bravery in speaking to Gary O'Toole exposed George Gibney and changed the course of my life for the better.

Gary O'Toole, you shone a light into the darkest corner of my past and gave up life as you knew it to expose Gibney. How lucky am I to call you my friend?

Johnny Watterson, you spoke for me in the *Sunday Tribune* when I could not, and Peter Murtagh, I will forever be grateful to you for having the courage to print Johnny's story.

Ber Carley, 'Susan', Loraine and all my fellow

survivors, those who came forward and those who did not, together we stand tall.

Mark Horgan, your humour, honesty and integrity made chatting to you for the podcast so much more enjoyable than it should have been. You'll be pleased to note that despite my initial resistance you did make it into my saved numbers.

Ciaran Cassidy, Second Captains and BBC Five Live, you gave my voice a platform and brought the story of George Gibney to a worldwide audience. Thank you also to the many other journalists who have not forgotten us over the years and have continued to keep our story alive in print.

To my friends, with whom I have laughed, cried and enjoyed more than my fair share of wine over the years. Orla, Sheila and Derek who stuck with me during my swimming years in Trojan. Jeannine, my nursing pal, bridesmaid and forever friend. The 'Desperate Housewives', Theresa, Maureen and Doreen, what days and nights we have shared. 'Tric's Party' group, Mary-Anne, Peggy and Mary, how we have laughed. Eimer, the source of most of those laughs. Fiona, who is kindness personified. Rob, who came to my rescue and managed to take at least one decent photo of me. Elaine, my golfing companion, with a tremendous capacity to listen and care. Kelly, who I can always rely on. Deirdre, baking queen and the mother my children think I should be. Calie, my counsellor, walking companion and friend. Olive and Kathryn, with whom I've shared a lifetime of happiness, tears and friendship.

Daniel, the young guardian angel on my shoulder and his mother Majella, my walking companion for thirty years, whose courage and strength is a daily dose of inspiration.

And so, to my family. Mum, with her inherent strength, kindness and courage. Dad, who showered me with love and taught me lessons that have lasted my lifetime. Eileen, godmother, cousin and pseudo-sister, who has held my hand from my earliest days and continues to do so. Doris and Caroline, my sisters, who were in my corner and fought for me when I needed them most. Ben, my big brother who is all that a big brother should be. And Michael my younger brother and childhood pal, who inhabits my soul.

Eamonn, my dearest friend and companion. You have loved me every step of the way, even when I couldn't love myself. Without your quiet strength I would never have got this far.

And finally, Aoife, Tiarnán, Naoise, Caoimhe and Jamie, who have completed my story. As I look at them daily, I think ... this is the future I dared to dream of.